Table of Contents

Introduction 5
Diverse Ways to Express Love Globally 5
Cross-Cultural Impact of Valentine's Day 8
Unity in Diversity: Love Beyond Boundaries 11

Chapter 1: Valentine's Day Around the World 15
Unique Celebrations in Different Countries 15
Cross-Cultural Influences on Love Traditions 21
Globalization of Valentine's Day Practices 27
Shared Themes in International Celebrations 32

Chapter 2: Cultural Adaptations and Traditions 37
Diverse Customs: Love Across Cultures 37
Local Influences Shaping Valentine's Day Celebrations 43
Embracing and Transforming Western Traditions 49
Fusion of Local and Global Love Symbols 55

Chapter 3: Global Icons of Love and Romance 60
International Symbols in the Language of Love 60
Shared Cultural References in Global Romanticism 65
Icons Crossing Cultural Barriers 70
Enduring Global Symbols of Love 75

Chapter 4: Controversies and Criticisms Worldwide 80
Cultural Debates on Valentine's Day Observance 80
Resisting and Reinterpreting Western Influences 85
Critiques on the Commercialization of Love 90
Balancing Global Trends with Cultural Identity 95

Chapter 5: Love Across Time and Cultures............100
Historical Perspectives on Global Love Traditions 100
Timeless Themes in Cross-Cultural Love Stories...................105
Love as a Universal Human Experience................................110
Influence of Ancient Cultures on Modern Love...................... 115

Chapter 6: Modern Global Love Trends 121
Technological Influences on International Romance............ 121
Social Media's Role in Cross-Cultural Connections...............127
Globalization of Dating Practices 133
Influence of Western Media on Global Love Trends..............139

Chapter 7: Global Perspectives on Long-Distance Love 144
Navigating Love Across Borders and Oceans 144
Cross-Cultural Challenges in Long-Distance Relationships .150
Shared Experiences in International Long-Distance Love ...156
Virtual Celebrations and Connecting Beyond Boundaries ...162

Conclusion: Love Knows No Borders 168
Uniting Humanity Through Love Celebrations.....................168
Shared Symbolism of Love Across Cultures 173
Embracing a Global Vision of Valentine's Day......................178

Glossary...184
Potential References.. 187

Copyright © 2024 by Blaze X. Maverick (Author)

All rights reserved. This book or any portion thereof may not be reproduced or used in any manner whatsoever without the express written permission of the publisher except for the use of brief quotations in a book review.

This book is copyright protected. This is only for personal use. You cannot amend, distributor, sell, use, quote or paraphrase any part or the content within this book without the consent of the author.

Please note the information contained within this document is for educational and entertainment purposes only. Every attempt has been made to provide accurate, up to date and reliable complete information. No warranties of any kind are expressed or implied. Readers acknowledge that the author is not engaging in the rendering of legal, financial, medical or professional advice. The content of this book has been derived from various sources. Please consult a licensed professional before attempting any techniques outlined in this book.

By reading this document, the readers agree that under no circumstances are the author responsible for any losses, direct or indirect, which are incurred as a result of the use of information contained within this document, including but not limited to errors, omissions or inaccuracies.

Thank you very much for reading this book.

Title: Celebrating Love Across Borders
Subtitle: Controversies and Criticisms Worldwide

Series: Eternal Valentine: Stories of Enduring Love: From Ancient Traditions to Modern Expressions
Author: Blaze X. Maverick

Introduction
Diverse Ways to Express Love Globally

In a world rich with cultural diversity, love manifests in a myriad of expressions, transcending geographical and social boundaries. This book embarks on a journey to explore the intricate tapestry of love on a global scale, delving into the unique ways different cultures celebrate and express this timeless emotion. As we venture into the heart of Valentine's Day, our lens widens to encompass not only the joyous festivities but also the controversies and criticisms that echo across borders.

Love, a universal language spoken in countless dialects, finds its resonance in the diverse ways people express their affection, devotion, and commitment across the globe. Each culture weaves its own narrative, blending tradition with modernity to create a rich mosaic of love rituals and customs.

In the enchanting landscapes of Japan, love is often expressed through the delicate art of origami, where meticulously folded paper cranes symbolize commitment and longevity. In contrast, the vibrant colors of India's Holi festival become a canvas for expressing love, as people playfully throw colored powders, breaking down social barriers and embracing the spirit of unity.

Across the Atlantic, in the heart of Europe, the love locks adorning bridges serve as tangible symbols of enduring affection. Couples etch their names onto padlocks, locking them onto bridges and throwing away the key, a metaphor for an unbreakable bond that defies the passage of time.

In parts of Africa, love is celebrated through dance, with rhythmic movements and vibrant beats telling stories of courtship and unity. The intricacies of traditional dances become a canvas for expressing emotions that words alone cannot capture.

The Middle East, with its rich tapestry of history and culture, often expresses love through intricate calligraphy. Poems and love letters adorned with elegant Arabic script convey the depth of emotions, while the symbolism of the hamsa, a hand-shaped amulet, wards off the evil eye, protecting the love it encompasses.

As we traverse the continents, we encounter countless variations of love expressed through food, music, art, and rituals. In South Korea, the 14th of every month holds a special significance, with different days dedicated to various expressions of love, from the romantic to the familial. Meanwhile, in Mexico, the tradition of serenading, known as "Las Mañanitas," adds a melodic touch to declarations of love under the moonlit sky.

The global kaleidoscope of love is not limited to romantic partnerships. Familial bonds are celebrated in various ways, from the honoring of ancestors during China's Qingming Festival to the joyous gatherings of family and friends during Thanksgiving in the United States.

This exploration of diverse expressions of love globally is a testament to the richness of human connection. In the chapters that follow, we will unravel the cross-cultural influences on love traditions, witness the fusion of local and global symbols, and delve into the controversies that have sparked debates on the celebration of love worldwide. As we navigate this intricate terrain, we invite you to open your heart to the beauty and complexity of love's many forms, transcending borders and embracing the shared human experience that unites us all.

Cross-Cultural Impact of Valentine's Day

In our exploration of love's global tapestry, we now turn our attention to the cross-cultural impact of Valentine's Day, a day that transcends its historical origins and has woven itself into the fabric of diverse societies around the world. As we navigate the nuances of this internationally celebrated day of love, we uncover the ways in which cultures adapt, reinterpret, and integrate this tradition into their own unique narratives.

Valentine's Day, with its roots in both ancient Roman and Christian traditions, has evolved into a global phenomenon that extends far beyond its Western origins. The romantic allure of the day has found resonance in cultures worldwide, sparking both adoration and critique as it mingles with local customs.

In the bustling streets of Paris, the city of love, Valentine's Day takes on an enchanting quality. The French embrace the day with an air of sophistication, exchanging beautifully crafted cards known as "cartes d'amour" and indulging in sumptuous meals at quaint bistros. The iconic Eiffel Tower becomes a symbol of love, illuminated in a warm glow that bathes the city in a romantic ambiance.

Moving eastward, in Japan, the celebration of love takes a unique turn. Here, Valentine's Day is observed in two parts. On February 14th, women express their affection by gifting chocolates to men. A month later, on White Day, men reciprocate with gifts, creating a harmonious exchange of love that extends beyond a single day.

In South Korea, Valentine's Day is not confined to romantic love alone. The 14th of every month holds a distinct significance, with each month dedicated to different expressions of love. From the romantic gestures of February to the celebration of friendship in May, this cultural adaptation of Valentine's Day reflects a multifaceted approach to love, encompassing various relationships.

India, a land of vibrant traditions, has embraced Valentine's Day with a blend of modernity and cultural richness. While the younger generation exchanges flowers, cards, and gifts, some regions also incorporate traditional elements. In Rajasthan, for instance, the festival of Basant Panchami coincides with Valentine's Day, infusing the celebration with a cultural tapestry of music and dance.

The impact of Valentine's Day in diverse cultures is not merely about the exchange of gifts and expressions of love; it also intertwines with local customs and values. In China, the celebration of love aligns with the Qixi Festival, a time when couples gather to pray for happiness and prosperity. The fusion of traditional festivities with the modern influence of Valentine's Day creates a unique and harmonious celebration.

While many cultures seamlessly integrate Valentine's Day into their traditions, others grapple with the influx of Western ideals. In some parts of the Middle East, where conservative values may clash with the perceived extravagance of Valentine's Day, the celebration has faced resistance. Nevertheless, pockets of the population embrace the day, finding creative ways to express love within the bounds of their cultural norms.

The cross-cultural impact of Valentine's Day is not without its controversies. In some regions, the commercialization of love has sparked debates about cultural authenticity and the intrusion of Western influences. As we navigate these complexities, we delve into the ways in which cultures navigate the fine line between adopting a global celebration and preserving their unique identities.

In the chapters that follow, we will explore the diverse customs that have emerged as a result of this cross-cultural exchange, witnessing the fusion of local and global love symbols. From the intricate rituals of courtship in Africa to the fusion of Western and indigenous traditions in the Americas, the impact of Valentine's Day continues to shape and reshape the expression of love on a global scale. As we embark on this journey, we invite you to unravel the layers of cultural adaptation, critique, and celebration that define the cross-cultural impact of Valentine's Day.

Unity in Diversity: Love Beyond Boundaries

As we embark on this exploration of love's global dimensions, we now delve into the profound theme of "Unity in Diversity: Love Beyond Boundaries." Love, a force that transcends borders and defies categorization, serves as a unifying thread in the rich tapestry of human experience. In this section, we navigate through the myriad expressions of love that bridge cultural, geographical, and social divides, illustrating the resilience and universality of this remarkable emotion.

Love, the most profound and intricate emotion known to humanity, emerges as a common thread weaving through the diverse landscapes of our world. It knows no boundaries, no borders, and it embraces the rich tapestry of human experience in all its complexities. As we celebrate love across borders, we encounter stories that embody the unity found within the diversity of global expressions of affection.

In the heart of Africa, love dances to the rhythmic beats of tradition. Across the continent, diverse communities celebrate love through vibrant rituals, from the energetic dances of the Maasai people to the intricate beadwork that tells tales of courtship and commitment. Here, love extends beyond the romantic to encompass family, community, and the connection to ancestral roots.

Journeying to the Americas, we witness the fusion of indigenous traditions with the global celebration of love. Native

American communities incorporate their unique ceremonies and symbols into Valentine's Day, creating a tapestry where ancient wisdom and contemporary romance intertwine. Love, in these contexts, becomes a bridge between generations, a continuation of cultural heritage.

Asia, with its vast diversity of cultures, showcases a myriad of ways love is expressed. In the bustling streets of India, the festival of Diwali becomes a celebration of love and light, as families come together to share joy and blessings. In China, the Qixi Festival, also known as the Chinese Valentine's Day, intertwines tales of celestial love with contemporary expressions of affection.

The Middle East, often depicted through a lens of complexity, reveals a tapestry of love stories that defy stereotypes. From the enduring tales of love found in Arabic poetry to the modern expressions of affection within the bounds of cultural norms, the Middle East paints a nuanced portrait of love that resonates with the universal quest for connection.

Europe, with its diverse array of languages and traditions, unites in the language of love. From the poetic gestures of Shakespearean England to the passionate flamenco dances of Spain, love transcends linguistic and cultural barriers, becoming a universal force that binds people together. The shared embrace of romance echoes through medieval castles, bustling cities, and quaint villages alike.

As we navigate the diverse expressions of love, it becomes evident that while cultural nuances color the canvas of affection, the underlying emotions are universal. Whether expressed through the intricate rituals of Japan, the passionate dances of Latin America, or the poetic verses of the Middle East, love resonates as a language that connects us all.

In exploring love beyond boundaries, we encounter narratives that defy societal expectations and challenge preconceived notions. LGBTQ+ communities around the world navigate the complexities of love, transcending cultural norms and forging their paths to acceptance and recognition. Love, in these contexts, becomes a powerful force for societal change, breaking down barriers and fostering inclusivity.

The celebration of love is not confined to romantic relationships alone; it extends to familial bonds, friendships, and the collective human experience. Festivals and traditions centered around love become moments of unity, where individuals from diverse backgrounds come together to honor the shared emotions that make us human.

In the chapters that follow, we will unravel the unique celebrations of love in different countries, exploring the global icons that transcend cultural barriers, and delving into the controversies that arise when love encounters societal norms. As we navigate this intricate terrain, we invite you to open your heart to the unity found within the diversity of global expressions of love, reminding us that, in the end, love knows no boundaries.

Chapter 1: Valentine's Day Around the World
Unique Celebrations in Different Countries

Valentine's Day, a day traditionally associated with love and romance, unfolds its narrative in diverse and distinctive ways as it traverses the globe. In this chapter, we embark on a journey to explore the unique celebrations of Valentine's Day in different countries, discovering the cultural nuances and traditions that color the universal theme of love.

Japan: Chocolates and Obligations

In the Land of the Rising Sun, Valentine's Day takes on a distinctive twist. Here, the day is marked by a tradition where women take the lead in expressing their affection. Women, ranging from friends to romantic interests, gift chocolates to the men in their lives. However, this act is not limited to expressions of love; it also includes obligatory chocolates known as "giri-choco," given to colleagues, friends, or even bosses as a gesture of courtesy and social obligation. The tradition continues a month later on White Day, when men reciprocate with gifts for the women who gifted them chocolates.

France: The Epitome of Romance

Renowned as the city of love, Paris sets the stage for a romantic spectacle on Valentine's Day. French lovers exchange "cartes d'amour," intricately designed love cards, often accompanied by handwritten poems expressing affection. The iconic Eiffel Tower becomes the centerpiece of the celebration, bathed in a warm glow, providing a picturesque backdrop for couples strolling along the Seine River. Romantic dinners at charming bistros and exchanging tokens of love encapsulate the essence of French romance on this special day.

South Korea: Love Celebrated Every Month

In South Korea, Valentine's Day isn't confined to a single day of celebration. Each month holds a distinct significance for expressions of love. February marks the traditional romantic gestures, while March is dedicated to the celebration of White Day, where men reciprocate the affections received. As the months progress, love is celebrated in various forms, from the appreciation of roses in May to the acknowledgment of the elderly in September. This unique approach to Valentine's Day reflects a holistic perspective on love, encompassing different relationships and aspects of life.

Italy: A Day for Lovers and Friends

Italy, a country steeped in romance and history, celebrates Valentine's Day with a focus on both romantic love and friendship. The day is not limited to couples; friends also exchange gifts and tokens of appreciation. The city of Verona, famously known as the setting for Shakespeare's "Romeo and Juliet," hosts events and festivals, drawing visitors from around the world to celebrate the universal theme of love in the city that epitomizes its enduring spirit.

Brazil: Celebration of Love and Affection

In Brazil, Valentine's Day, known as "Dia dos Namorados," is celebrated on June 12th, aligning with the eve of Saint Anthony's Day, the marriage saint. The day is marked by exchanging gifts, romantic dinners, and declarations of love. Brazilians celebrate not only romantic love but also the broader concept of affection, extending the festivities to include friends and family. This inclusive approach transforms the day into a celebration of love in all its forms.

India: Blending Tradition with Modernity

In the diverse cultural landscape of India, Valentine's Day has found a place among the younger generation. While traditional customs vary across regions, the celebration of love has gained popularity, especially in urban areas. Young couples exchange flowers, cards, and gifts, embracing the modern aspects of Valentine's Day while incorporating traditional elements. Some regions, like Rajasthan, see the festival of Basant Panchami coinciding with Valentine's Day, infusing the celebration with a cultural tapestry of music and dance.

Denmark: Gaekkebrev and Playful Affection

In Denmark, Valentine's Day is marked by the exchange of "gaekkebrev," or joking letters. These letters are anonymous, containing playful rhymes and intricate cutout designs. The sender's identity is concealed, and the recipient must guess who sent the letter. If the recipient correctly guesses the sender, they receive an Easter egg as a reward. This lighthearted and playful tradition adds a unique twist to the celebration of love in Denmark.

China: Qixi Festival and Celestial Love

In China, Valentine's Day is intertwined with the Qixi Festival, also known as the Double Seventh Festival. Celebrated on the seventh day of the seventh lunar month, the festival has ancient roots and tells the tale of star-crossed lovers, Zhinü and Niulang, who are only allowed to meet once a year. Traditionally, young women display their domestic skills on this day, symbolizing their readiness for marriage. The celebration reflects a blend of mythology and cultural practices, creating a unique tapestry of love in the Chinese context.

United States: Roses, Chocolates, and Romantic Gestures

In the United States, Valentine's Day is marked by the exchange of romantic gestures, flowers, and chocolates. The iconic red roses become symbols of love, and couples often indulge in romantic dinners and special activities. Greeting cards, expressing sentiments ranging from affection to humor, are exchanged widely. While the celebration may vary from a quiet dinner at home to elaborate surprises, the essence remains a celebration of love and appreciation.

Mexico: Serenades and Declarations of Love

In Mexico, the celebration of love extends beyond a single day. The week leading up to Valentine's Day, known as "Semana de Amor," is filled with festivities. Couples exchange flowers, chocolates, and heartfelt messages. One of the traditional customs involves serenading, where mariachi bands or individuals express love through music. The festive atmosphere and declarations of love create a lively and passionate celebration in Mexican culture.

Australia: Love in the Southern Hemisphere

In the Southern Hemisphere, where February is summer, Valentine's Day takes on a different flavor. Australians celebrate with outdoor activities, picnics, and beach outings. The warm weather becomes a backdrop for romantic gestures, from leisurely walks in the park to adventurous activities. The unique climate adds a distinctive touch to the celebration of love in the land Down Under.

Egypt: A Blend of Ancient and Modern Love

In Egypt, Valentine's Day has found its place in the hearts of the younger generation. While the celebration may not align with traditional Egyptian customs, it has become popular among urban youth. The day is marked by the exchange of gifts, flowers, and romantic gestures, reflecting a blend of ancient history and modern expressions of love.

Conclusion: A Tapestry of Global Love Celebrations

As we traverse the diverse celebrations of Valentine's Day around the world, a rich tapestry of love unfolds. From the poetic gestures in France to the playful traditions in Denmark, each country adds its unique colors to the universal theme of love. Valentine's Day, in its global journey, becomes a mirror reflecting the cultural nuances, historical influences, and contemporary expressions of affection that make love a truly transcendent force. In the chapters that follow, we will explore the cross-cultural influences on love traditions, the fusion of local and global symbols, and the controversies that arise when love encounters societal norms. Join us as we continue our exploration of love's journey across borders, embracing the beauty and diversity that define the celebration of love around the world.

Cross-Cultural Influences on Love Traditions

In the kaleidoscope of global celebrations, Valentine's Day undergoes a fascinating transformation as it encounters diverse cultures. This chapter delves into the intricate web of cross-cultural influences that shape love traditions around the world, exploring how this Western-originated celebration has been embraced, adapted, and interwoven with local customs.

Japan: Blending Tradition with Modern Romance

In Japan, the celebration of Valentine's Day is a fascinating interplay of ancient tradition and modern romance. While the Western influence is evident in the exchange of chocolates, the tradition has taken on a unique form. Women, both romantically involved and socially obligated, present beautifully crafted chocolates to men. The concept of "giri-choco," or obligation chocolate, adds a layer of complexity, reflecting the influence of societal expectations on this global celebration. The subsequent celebration of White Day, where men reciprocate with gifts, further exemplifies the fusion of Western and Japanese customs.

China: Qixi Festival and the Celestial Romance

China's celebration of love on Valentine's Day is intertwined with the Qixi Festival, a traditional Chinese festival known as the Double Seventh Festival. The Qixi Festival originated from the mythological tale of the Weaver Girl and the Cowherd, star-crossed lovers separated by the Milky Way. The celestial romance of Qixi adds a unique layer to the celebration, blending ancient mythology with modern expressions of affection. The festival has become a harmonious fusion of traditional customs and the global celebration of love.

South Korea: Love Celebrated Every Month

In South Korea, the celebration of love on Valentine's Day extends beyond a singular day, creating a tapestry of expressions throughout the year. Each month holds a unique significance, from romantic gestures in February to the celebration of friendship in May. This multifaceted approach to love reflects a cultural adaptation that seamlessly integrates global influences with local values. The Korean celebration becomes a dynamic fusion of traditional and modern expressions of affection.

Brazil: Merging Western and Indigenous Influences

In Brazil, the celebration of love on Valentine's Day, known as "Dia dos Namorados," merges Western traditions with indigenous influences. The day aligns with the eve of Saint Anthony's Day, the marriage saint, creating a unique blend of Catholic and indigenous beliefs. The festivities extend beyond romantic love to encompass familial and platonic relationships, reflecting the inclusive nature of Brazilian culture. This amalgamation of cultural influences transforms the celebration into a vibrant expression of love in its various forms.

Italy: Romance and History Intertwined

Italy, with its rich history and reputation as a bastion of romance, adds its own touch to the celebration of love. While embracing the global aspects of Valentine's Day, Italians infuse the celebration with historical and cultural significance. The city of Verona, associated with Shakespeare's "Romeo and Juliet," becomes a focal point for romantic events, intertwining contemporary expressions of love with the echoes of the past. The celebration reflects Italy's ability to seamlessly weave global traditions into its cultural tapestry.

India: Traditional Customs in a Modern Context

In India, Valentine's Day has found a place within the vast tapestry of cultural diversity. While traditional customs vary across regions, the celebration has gained popularity, especially among the younger generation. The adaptation of Valentine's Day into the Indian context showcases the dynamic nature of cultural influences. Young couples exchange flowers, cards, and gifts, embracing the modern aspects of Valentine's Day while incorporating traditional elements. The celebration becomes a harmonious fusion of global and local expressions of affection.

Middle East: Navigating Cultural Sensitivities

The celebration of Valentine's Day in the Middle East reflects the delicate balance between embracing global traditions and respecting cultural sensitivities. In some conservative regions, the day may be met with resistance due to perceived extravagance and Western influences. However, pockets of the population choose to participate in the celebration, adapting it to align with local customs. This juxtaposition highlights the ongoing negotiation between global celebrations and the preservation of cultural identity in the Middle East.

United States: Global Icons and Local Celebrations

In the United States, Valentine's Day has become a global phenomenon with cultural influences flowing in both directions. While the day is celebrated in a manner consistent with Western traditions, the global exchange of ideas has introduced new elements. The symbolism of red roses, heart-shaped chocolates, and greeting cards has transcended borders, becoming universal symbols of love. The celebration in the U.S. reflects the reciprocal nature of cultural influence, where global icons become part of local celebrations.

Mexico: Serenades and Cultural Synthesis

Mexico's celebration of Valentine's Day is a vibrant example of cultural synthesis. The festivities, extending beyond a single day, involve the exchange of flowers, chocolates, and heartfelt messages. Traditional customs, such as serenading, add a unique Mexican touch to the celebration. The fusion of global and indigenous traditions creates a celebration that resonates with both modern expressions of love and the rich cultural heritage of Mexico.

Australia: A Southern Hemisphere Perspective

In the Southern Hemisphere, where February is summer, Valentine's Day takes on a unique character. Australians celebrate with outdoor activities, picnics, and beach outings. The warm weather becomes a backdrop for romantic gestures, from leisurely walks in the park to adventurous activities. The celebration reflects not only the influence of global traditions but also the adaptation of those traditions to fit the local climate and lifestyle.

Egypt: Global Celebrations in an Ancient Land

In Egypt, Valentine's Day has found resonance among the younger generation, illustrating the global impact of this celebration in an ancient land. While the day may not align with traditional Egyptian customs, it has become popular among urban youth. The celebration involves the exchange of gifts, flowers, and romantic gestures, reflecting a blend of ancient history and modern expressions of love. Egypt's adaptation of Valentine's Day showcases the universality of love as a cross-cultural force.

Conclusion: Love as a Cultural Kaleidoscope

As we explore the cross-cultural influences on love traditions, Valentine's Day emerges as a cultural kaleidoscope, reflecting the dynamic interplay between global and local expressions of affection. From the poetic gestures in France to the multifaceted celebrations in South Korea, each country adds its unique hues to the canvas of love. The chapters that follow will continue this exploration, unraveling the global icons that transcend cultural barriers and delving into the controversies that arise when love encounters societal norms. Join us as we navigate the intricate terrain of love's journey across borders, appreciating the beauty and diversity that define the celebration of love around the world.

Globalization of Valentine's Day Practices

In the interconnected world of the 21st century, cultural exchange has become a hallmark of globalization, and few celebrations illustrate this as vividly as Valentine's Day. Originally rooted in Western traditions, Valentine's Day has traversed borders and transcended cultural boundaries, becoming a global phenomenon celebrated in diverse ways across continents. This chapter explores the globalization of Valentine's Day practices, tracing the evolution of this celebration as it journeys through cultures and adapts to the dynamics of a globalized world.

The Western Origins: A Love Story Spreads

Valentine's Day, as we know it today, finds its roots in Western traditions, with historical ties to both Roman and Christian cultures. The celebration gained popularity in Europe during the Middle Ages and later evolved into a day dedicated to romantic love. In the 19th century, the exchange of love notes and cards became a hallmark of Valentine's Day in Western societies. Initially confined to this regional context, the global journey of Valentine's Day began to take shape with the advent of globalization.

The Rise of Global Icons: Roses, Chocolates, and Cupids

As Valentine's Day transcended borders, certain symbols and traditions became global icons, universally recognized and embraced. The exchange of red roses, heart-shaped chocolates, and Cupid's arrows became synonymous with the celebration of love. These symbols, rooted in Western imagery, found resonance across cultures, shaping a shared visual language of affection. The globalization of these iconic elements reflects the power of imagery in transcending cultural and linguistic barriers.

Global Influence on Local Traditions: Adaptations and Blends

One of the fascinating aspects of the globalization of Valentine's Day is the adaptability of local traditions to incorporate global influences. Countries around the world have seamlessly integrated Western practices with their own cultural expressions of love. In Japan, for example, the tradition of women gifting chocolates on Valentine's Day has been embraced, but with a unique twist, reflecting both local customs and the global influence of the celebration. Similarly, South Korea's multifaceted approach to Valentine's Day, celebrating different forms of love each month, showcases the adaptability of the global celebration to diverse cultural contexts.

Commercialization of Love: A Global Industry

As Valentine's Day traversed the globe, it became not only a celebration of love but also a significant economic force. The commercialization of love, a phenomenon often associated with Western consumer culture, has become a global industry. From the sale of greeting cards and flowers to the marketing of romantic getaways and special events, businesses around the world capitalize on the sentiments associated with Valentine's

Day. This commercial aspect highlights the impact of globalization not only on cultural practices but also on economic landscapes worldwide.

Social Media's Role: A Global Platform for Affection

The advent of social media has further accelerated the globalization of Valentine's Day practices. Platforms like Instagram, Facebook, and Twitter provide a global stage for individuals to share their expressions of love. From sharing romantic photos to declaring affection in public posts, social media has become a digital canvas for global celebrations of love. The influence of Western media and trends on these platforms contributes to a shared global experience of Valentine's Day, creating a virtual space for the exchange of affectionate gestures.

Cultural Fusion and Synthesis: A Two-Way Street

While Valentine's Day has undeniably influenced and been embraced by cultures worldwide, the process of globalization is not unidirectional. Cultural fusion and synthesis are dynamic processes, and as Valentine's Day becomes a global celebration, it also undergoes transformations shaped by diverse cultural influences. In some cases, local traditions and customs influence the way Valentine's Day is celebrated, adding unique flavors to the global celebration. This two-way exchange exemplifies the reciprocal nature of cultural globalization.

Controversies and Resistance: Globalization's Backlash

The globalization of Valentine's Day has not been without its controversies and resistance. In some cultures and regions, the celebration has faced opposition due to perceived Westernization, commercialization, or clashes with local values. Debates on the appropriateness of embracing a Western celebration, especially one associated with romantic love, highlight the tensions that can arise when global practices encounter deeply rooted cultural norms. The controversies surrounding Valentine's Day provide a lens through which to examine the complexities of cultural globalization.

Virtual Connections: Love Across Digital Borders

The digital age has brought about new dimensions to the globalization of Valentine's Day, especially in the realm of long-distance relationships. Virtual celebrations, facilitated by technology, allow individuals separated by geographical borders to connect and share the experience of Valentine's Day. From virtual dates to online gift exchanges, the digital space has become a bridge for love that transcends physical boundaries.

Cultural Appropriation: Navigating Sensitivities

The globalization of Valentine's Day also raises questions about cultural appropriation and sensitivity. As the celebration spreads to diverse cultures, it becomes essential to navigate the fine line between appreciating and appropriating local traditions. Awareness of cultural nuances and the respectful incorporation of global practices into local contexts are crucial considerations in the process of cultural globalization.

Conclusion: Love's Global Tapestry

In tracing the globalization of Valentine's Day practices, we witness the evolution of a celebration that transcends its Western origins to become a global tapestry of love. The shared symbols, commercial aspects, and digital expressions create a common ground for individuals around the world. Yet, the dynamic nature of cultural globalization ensures that the celebration is not a monolithic entity but a mosaic of diverse influences and adaptations. As we delve into the chapters that follow, we will explore the cross-cultural impact of Valentine's Day, the diverse ways love is expressed globally, and the controversies that arise in this intricate interplay of love and cultural exchange. Join us as we continue our exploration of love's journey across borders, appreciating the interconnectedness that defines the celebration of love around the world.

Shared Themes in International Celebrations

Valentine's Day, though celebrated across diverse cultures, shares common threads that weave through the tapestry of global expressions of love. As this chapter explores the international celebrations of Valentine's Day, we delve into the shared themes that transcend borders, unifying people in the universal language of affection and romance.

Expressions of Affection: The Heartfelt Essence

At the heart of Valentine's Day celebrations worldwide lies the fundamental theme of expressing affection. Whether through the exchange of gifts, words, or gestures, individuals across cultures use this day to convey their love and appreciation for one another. The essence of expressing affection is a universal theme that connects people, transcending linguistic and cultural differences.

Symbolism of Love: Roses, Hearts, and Cupids

Certain symbols have become iconic representations of love and are widely shared across cultures during Valentine's Day celebrations. The red rose, with its rich symbolism of passion and romance, is exchanged as a token of love in many countries. Heart-shaped chocolates and decorations adorn the celebration, embodying the universal symbol of love. Cupid, the winged cherub associated with love and desire in Western mythology, has also transcended cultural boundaries to become a shared symbol of Valentine's Day worldwide.

Romantic Gestures: Dinner Dates and Special Moments

The celebration of love often involves romantic gestures that create memorable moments. Across continents, couples engage in special activities such as romantic dinners, outings, or surprise events to express their love. The concept of dedicating a day to spend quality time together, fostering connection and intimacy, is a shared theme that resonates in Valentine's Day celebrations globally.

Gift Exchanges: Tokens of Love and Appreciation

The tradition of exchanging gifts on Valentine's Day is a common theme that binds celebrations worldwide. From small tokens of affection to elaborate presents, the act of giving gifts is a way to express love and appreciation. The sentiment behind gift-giving is shared among cultures, emphasizing the thought and effort put into selecting a meaningful expression of love for a partner, friend, or family member.

Celebrating Relationships Beyond Romantic Love

While Valentine's Day is often associated with romantic love, its celebration extends beyond romantic relationships. The broader theme of celebrating love in all its forms is a shared aspect of international celebrations. Friends, family members, and even colleagues exchange tokens of affection, emphasizing the diverse relationships that contribute to the richness of the human experience.

Festive Atmosphere: Decorations and Ambiance

Valentine's Day brings with it a festive atmosphere characterized by vibrant decorations, romantic ambiance, and an overall sense of joy. This shared theme manifests in various forms, from the streets of Paris adorned with romantic lighting to the vibrant festivals in Brazil. The creation of a festive atmosphere contributes to the sense of community and shared celebration during Valentine's Day.

Incorporation of Romantic Imagery: Art and Media

The imagery associated with romance and love, propagated through art and media, is a shared theme in international Valentine's Day celebrations. From romantic movies and music to literature and visual arts, the celebration draws on a global pool of romantic imagery. This shared cultural reservoir influences the way individuals perceive and express love during Valentine's Day.

Emphasis on Love's Timelessness: Ancient and Modern Influences

Valentine's Day often incorporates elements that emphasize the timeless nature of love. In various celebrations, there is a recognition of love's enduring qualities, drawing inspiration from both ancient traditions and modern expressions. This fusion of the old and the new creates a sense of continuity and universality in the celebration of love.

Culinary Delights: Special Treats for Loved Ones

The celebration of love often extends to the culinary realm, with special treats and delicacies becoming a shared theme. Whether it's heart-shaped chocolates, romantic dinners, or the exchange of favorite foods, the culinary aspect of

Valentine's Day reflects the global appreciation for indulging in delightful experiences with loved ones.

Poetic Expressions: Words of Love and Affection

The tradition of conveying love through poetic expressions is a shared theme that transcends cultural boundaries. Whether through handwritten letters, romantic cards, or heartfelt poems, individuals around the world use words to articulate their feelings on Valentine's Day. This emphasis on the poetic and expressive nature of love adds a universal touch to the celebration.

Cultural Adaptations: Infusing Local Flavor

While shared themes unite Valentine's Day celebrations globally, there is also a beautiful diversity in the way each culture infuses its unique flavor into the celebration. Cultural adaptations, whether through traditional rituals, local customs, or regional symbols, add richness to the global celebration while maintaining a connection to individual cultural identities.

Conclusion: Love's Common Language

In exploring the shared themes in international celebrations of Valentine's Day, we discover the common language that unites people across the world in the celebration of love. The universal expressions of affection, iconic symbols, and shared rituals create a global tapestry of love that transcends geographical and cultural boundaries. As we journey through the chapters ahead, we will continue to unravel the intricacies of love's expression, exploring the cross-cultural impact of Valentine's Day and the controversies that arise when love encounters societal norms. Join us as we navigate the intricate terrain of love's journey across borders, appreciating the beauty and diversity that define the celebration of love around the world.

Chapter 2: Cultural Adaptations and Traditions
Diverse Customs: Love Across Cultures

Love, a universal emotion, finds expression in a myriad of customs and traditions that vary across cultures. In this chapter, we embark on a journey to explore the diverse customs that shape the celebration of love around the world. From ancient rituals to modern adaptations, these cultural expressions paint a rich tapestry of love that transcends borders.

Japan: The Artistry of Gift-Giving

In Japan, the celebration of love is intricately woven into the artistry of gift-giving, particularly during romantic occasions such as Valentine's Day. While Western influences introduced the concept of exchanging chocolates on Valentine's Day, Japan has adapted this tradition with a distinctive touch. Women express their affection by presenting handmade chocolates, showcasing creativity and effort. The act of gift-giving becomes a form of artistic expression, elevating the celebration to a nuanced cultural practice that blends modernity with traditional craftsmanship.

India: The Festive Fusion of Colors

In the diverse cultural landscape of India, expressions of love are intertwined with traditional festivals and rituals. Holi, the festival of colors, becomes a vibrant celebration of love and togetherness. Couples playfully smear each other with colorful powders, breaking down social barriers and fostering a sense of unity. This fusion of romantic expression with traditional festivities illustrates how love becomes an integral part of cultural celebrations in India, creating a unique and festive atmosphere.

Italy: The Language of Romance in Gestures

Italy, often considered a romantic haven, has a long history of poetic expressions of love. Beyond the global celebration of Valentine's Day, Italians convey affection through gestures deeply rooted in their cultural heritage. From the poetic serenades echoing through moonlit streets to the intricate language of hand gestures, love in Italy is not just a feeling but a cultural expression that permeates daily life. This emphasis on the subtle art of romantic gestures adds a layer of cultural richness to the celebration of love.

China: Ancient Symbols and Contemporary Love

China, with its rich cultural history, infuses ancient symbols into the celebration of love. Red, symbolizing luck and prosperity, becomes a prominent color in weddings and romantic events. Traditional symbols such as the Mandarin duck, a representation of love and fidelity, find their way into contemporary expressions of affection. The interplay between ancient symbols and modern love showcases China's ability to seamlessly blend tradition with the evolving landscape of romance.

Mexico: Music, Dance, and Passionate Expressions

In Mexico, the celebration of love is intertwined with vibrant music, dance, and passionate expressions. Traditional dances, such as the Jarabe Tapatío, become a lively celebration of courtship and affection. Music, particularly the soulful melodies of mariachi bands, sets the stage for romantic serenades. Love in Mexico is not confined to gestures; it is a sensory experience, a harmonious blend of rhythm and passion that reflects the cultural vibrancy of the country.

Ghana: The Symbolism of Beadwork and Courtship

In the rich cultural tapestry of Ghana, love is expressed through intricate beadwork, with each bead carrying symbolic meaning. Beads are woven into garments and accessories, telling stories of courtship, commitment, and familial bonds. The art of beadwork becomes a visual language, allowing individuals to convey their feelings and intentions. This cultural expression showcases how love is embedded in the craftsmanship and symbolism of traditional practices.

France: Romanticism in Every Gesture

France, renowned as the epitome of romance, celebrates love with an emphasis on poetic gestures and artistic expressions. From the elegant architecture of Paris to the romantic landscapes of Provence, every element of French culture contributes to the celebration of love. The exchange of handwritten letters, the appreciation of fine arts, and the enjoyment of culinary delights all become expressions of affection. Love in France is not just a sentiment; it is a way of life that embraces beauty and romance in every gesture.

South Korea: Traditions Beyond Valentine's Day

South Korea, with its multifaceted approach to love celebrations, extends the expression of affection beyond Valentine's Day. The celebration of Pepero Day on November 11th involves the exchange of chocolate-covered sticks, adding another layer to the cultural tapestry of love. Additionally, the celebration of White Day and the observance of Black Day for singles highlight the nuanced ways in which South Korea expresses and navigates the complexities of love throughout the year.

Native American Cultures: Sacred Symbolism and Rituals

Various Native American cultures express love through sacred symbolism and rituals. The exchange of handcrafted jewelry, adorned with symbols such as hearts, feathers, or animals, becomes a meaningful expression of affection. Rituals associated with courtship, often involving communal gatherings and dances, reinforce the communal aspect of love within Native American communities. These traditions highlight the interconnectedness of love with the natural world and community bonds.

Morocco: Courting Through Tea Ceremonies

In Morocco, love is often expressed through the art of tea ceremonies. The sharing of mint tea becomes a cultural practice associated with hospitality, courtship, and expressing affection. The preparation and presentation of tea involve intricate rituals, creating a space for meaningful conversations and connections. This cultural expression of love emphasizes the importance of shared moments and hospitality in romantic relationships.

Russia: The Symbolism of Matryoshka Dolls

In Russia, the celebration of love is intertwined with the symbolism of Matryoshka dolls. These nested dolls, with each layer revealing a smaller one inside, represent the idea of layers in a relationship and the unfolding of emotions. The exchange of Matryoshka dolls becomes a unique way to convey the depth and gradual revelation of feelings in romantic relationships. This cultural adaptation showcases how symbols deeply rooted in tradition can become poignant expressions of love.

Conclusion: Love's Cultural Mosaic

As we explore the diverse customs that shape the celebration of love across cultures, a rich mosaic emerges, reflecting the unique expressions and traditions that define each society. Love becomes not only a universal emotion but also a cultural tapestry woven with the threads of ancient rituals, modern adaptations, and regional symbolism. In the chapters that follow, we will continue to unravel the intricate layers of love's expression, exploring the impact of cultural adaptations on Valentine's Day celebrations worldwide. Join us as we navigate the cultural nuances that make love a beautifully diverse and universally cherished experience.

Local Influences Shaping Valentine's Day Celebrations

The celebration of Valentine's Day transcends its Western origins as it encounters the diverse cultures of the world. Local influences play a significant role in shaping the way love is celebrated, adding unique flavors and traditions to this global phenomenon. In this chapter, we delve into the cultural tapestry of love, exploring how local influences shape Valentine's Day celebrations across different regions.

Japan: Giri-Choco and Honmei-Choco

In Japan, the celebration of Valentine's Day takes on a nuanced form, influenced by both traditional customs and modern expressions of love. The practice of exchanging chocolates on Valentine's Day is deeply ingrained, but it has a unique twist. Women not only express romantic feelings through "honmei-choco" (true feeling chocolate) but also present "giri-choco" (obligation chocolate) to colleagues and friends. This blending of traditional obligation with modern romantic expression showcases how local influences shape the celebration of love in Japan, adding layers of complexity and cultural significance.

South Korea: Love Celebrated Every Month

South Korea's approach to Valentine's Day reflects the influence of local customs and societal expectations. The celebration extends beyond a single day, with each month holding significance for different forms of love. From Rose Day to Pepero Day, South Korea's unique calendar of love celebrations is shaped by both global influences and local cultural values. This multifaceted approach to expressing love illustrates how the fusion of tradition and modernity creates a distinct celebration that resonates with South Korean society.

Brazil: Dia dos Namorados and Saint Anthony's Day

In Brazil, the celebration of love on Valentine's Day, known as "Dia dos Namorados," is influenced by a fusion of Western traditions and local customs. The date aligns with the eve of Saint Anthony's Day, the marriage saint. This cultural amalgamation expands the celebration beyond romantic love to encompass familial and platonic relationships. The emphasis on inclusivity and the incorporation of local saints into the celebration highlight how Brazil shapes the global celebration of love with its unique cultural influences.

Italy: Verona, Romeo, and Juliet

Italy, with its rich cultural history and association with romance, infuses Valentine's Day with local influences that evoke the spirit of the country. The city of Verona, linked to Shakespeare's "Romeo and Juliet," becomes a focal point for romantic events. The celebration is not merely a globalized expression of love but a reflection of Italy's cultural heritage and historical significance. The blending of global symbols with local narratives transforms the celebration into a uniquely Italian expression of love.

India: Fusion of Traditional and Modern Elements

In India, the celebration of Valentine's Day is influenced by a blend of traditional customs and modern expressions of love. While traditional festivals like Holi and Diwali often involve romantic elements, Valentine's Day has found its place in the cultural tapestry. The exchange of flowers, cards, and gifts reflects a fusion of Western practices with the essence of Indian romance. The celebration becomes a dynamic interplay of tradition and modernity, showcasing how local influences shape the expression of love in India.

Middle East: Negotiating Cultural Sensitivities

In the Middle East, the celebration of Valentine's Day is shaped by the delicate balance between embracing global traditions and respecting cultural sensitivities. While some regions may resist the celebration due to perceived Westernization, others choose to participate, adapting it to align with local customs. This negotiation between global influences and cultural identity illustrates how the Middle East shapes Valentine's Day celebrations within the context of its unique cultural sensitivities.

United States: From Local Traditions to Global Icons

In the United States, Valentine's Day has evolved from local traditions to become a global phenomenon. The exchange of cards, chocolates, and flowers has become universal symbols of love. However, the celebration in the U.S. reflects a dynamic interplay between global icons and local customs. The emphasis on personal gestures, such as handwritten notes and thoughtful gifts, showcases how the celebration is shaped by both global trends and individual expressions of affection.

Mexico: Serenades and Cultural Synthesis

Mexico's celebration of love is influenced by a synthesis of Western traditions and indigenous customs. The festivities, extending beyond a single day, involve the exchange of flowers, chocolates, and heartfelt messages. Traditional customs, such as serenading, add a unique Mexican touch to the celebration. This fusion of global and indigenous traditions reflects how Mexico shapes the celebration of love, creating a cultural synthesis that resonates with the vibrant heritage of the country.

France: The Language of Love in Every Gesture

In France, the celebration of love is deeply intertwined with the country's cultural emphasis on romance and aesthetics. Beyond the global symbols of red roses and heart-shaped chocolates, the French celebrate love through a variety of nuanced gestures. From handwritten love letters to poetic expressions, every act becomes an artful expression of affection. France's influence on the global celebration lies not only in popular symbols but also in the refined and artistic ways love is expressed.

Australia: A Southern Hemisphere Perspective

In the Southern Hemisphere, where February is summer, Australia shapes the celebration of love with its unique climate and lifestyle. Valentine's Day becomes an opportunity for outdoor activities, picnics, and beach outings. The warm weather provides a backdrop for romantic gestures, blending global traditions with local adaptations that suit the Australian lifestyle. This Southern Hemisphere perspective adds a distinct flavor to the global celebration of love.

Egypt: Ancient Land Embracing Modern Celebrations

In Egypt, an ancient land, the celebration of Valentine's Day illustrates the global impact of this tradition in a historical context. While the day may not align with traditional Egyptian customs, it has gained popularity among urban youth. The celebration involves the exchange of gifts, flowers, and romantic gestures, showcasing the blending of ancient history with modern expressions of love. Egypt's adaptation of Valentine's Day reflects the universality of love as a cross-cultural force.

Conclusion: Love's Cultural Kaleidoscope

As we explore how local influences shape Valentine's Day celebrations around the world, a cultural kaleidoscope unfolds. Each region contributes unique hues and patterns to the global celebration of love, illustrating the dynamic interplay between tradition and modernity. Love, as expressed on Valentine's Day, becomes a reflection of cultural identity, historical narratives, and the negotiation between global trends and local customs. In the chapters that follow, we will continue to unravel the intricate layers of love's expression, exploring global icons, enduring symbols, and the controversies that arise when love encounters societal norms. Join us as we navigate the diverse landscapes of love, appreciating the beauty and complexity that define the celebration of love around the world.

Embracing and Transforming Western Traditions

The celebration of Valentine's Day, rooted in Western traditions, has undergone a fascinating journey as it encounters cultures around the world. In this chapter, we explore how different societies have embraced and transformed Western traditions, incorporating them into their own cultural tapestry. From Japan to Brazil, South Korea to Egypt, the global celebration of love reflects a dynamic interplay between Western influences and local adaptations.

Japan: Chocolates, Obligation, and Cultural Fusion

In Japan, the tradition of exchanging chocolates on Valentine's Day has been embraced with a unique twist. While the act of giving chocolates has its roots in Western practices, Japan has transformed this tradition into a multifaceted expression of affection. The concept of "giri-choco" (obligation chocolate) involves women giving chocolates to colleagues and friends, transcending the romantic gesture. This cultural fusion of Western customs with Japanese nuances showcases how traditions are embraced and transformed, creating a celebration that resonates with local values.

South Korea: A Calendar of Love Celebrations

South Korea has not only embraced Western traditions but has also transformed the celebration of love into a calendar of events throughout the year. From Valentine's Day to White Day and Pepero Day, each occasion brings unique customs and expressions of affection. The influence of Western practices is evident, but South Korea has shaped these traditions to align with its cultural values, creating a distinctive celebration that goes beyond the confines of a single day.

Brazil: Dia dos Namorados and the Blend of Traditions

In Brazil, the celebration of Valentine's Day, known as "Dia dos Namorados," has been embraced with a Brazilian twist. The fusion of Western practices with local customs, such as the celebration aligning with Saint Anthony's Day, reflects the dynamic way in which traditions are embraced and transformed. The blending of global icons with indigenous narratives creates a celebration that captures the essence of Brazilian culture while participating in the global celebration of love.

India: Traditional Festivals and Modern Expressions

In India, the celebration of Valentine's Day coexists with traditional festivals that have romantic elements. While the exchange of flowers, cards, and gifts aligns with Western traditions, India has seamlessly integrated these practices into its diverse cultural landscape. The celebration becomes a fusion of traditional customs with modern expressions of love, showcasing how Western traditions are embraced and transformed within the Indian context.

Egypt: Ancient Land Embracing Modernity

In Egypt, an ancient land with a rich historical tapestry, the celebration of Valentine's Day reflects the embrace of modern Western traditions. While the day may not align with ancient Egyptian customs, urban youth in Egypt have adopted the celebration, incorporating it into their contemporary lives. The exchange of gifts, flowers, and romantic gestures illustrates the transformative power of Western traditions in a cultural context deeply rooted in history.

China: From Traditional Symbols to Modern Expressions

China's celebration of love reflects a fusion of traditional symbols with modern Western practices. While red has deep cultural significance as a symbol of luck and prosperity, the exchange of gifts, particularly roses, aligns with Western traditions. China's approach illustrates the adaptability of cultural traditions, showcasing how ancient symbols seamlessly coexist with modern expressions of love.

Italy: Verona, Romeo, and Juliet as Global Icons

Italy, with its historical association with romance, has embraced and transformed Western traditions into global icons. The city of Verona, linked to Shakespeare's "Romeo and Juliet," has become synonymous with the celebration of love. While embracing global symbols like red roses and heart-shaped chocolates, Italy has transformed its cultural heritage into a celebration that transcends national borders, creating a timeless and universally recognized expression of love.

Middle East: Navigating Western Influences and Cultural Sensitivities

In the Middle East, the celebration of Valentine's Day involves a delicate negotiation between embracing Western influences and respecting cultural sensitivities. While some regions resist the celebration due to perceived Westernization, others choose to participate, adapting it to align with local customs. This complex interplay reflects how traditions are navigated within the context of cultural identity and sensitivities.

Australia: Western Traditions in a Southern Hemisphere Context

In Australia, a country in the Southern Hemisphere, Valentine's Day is celebrated in the warmth of summer. While adopting Western traditions such as the exchange of cards and gifts, Australians have transformed the celebration to suit their unique climate and lifestyle. Outdoor activities, picnics, and beach outings become a distinctive way of embracing Western traditions within the Australian context.

France: Elevating Western Symbols with French Elegance

France, known for its sophistication and emphasis on romance, has elevated Western symbols to embody French elegance. The exchange of love letters, romantic gestures, and appreciation for fine arts becomes a cultural expression that goes beyond the globalized symbols of love. France's transformation of Western traditions reflects not just an embrace but an enhancement of romantic expressions, adding a layer of refinement to the celebration of love.

Mexico: Serenades and Cultural Synthesis

In Mexico, the celebration of love involves a unique synthesis of Western traditions with indigenous customs. While adopting global practices like the exchange of flowers and chocolates, Mexico adds its own touch with traditions such as serenading. This cultural synthesis showcases how Western traditions are not merely embraced but integrated into the rich cultural tapestry of Mexico, creating a celebration that resonates with the vibrancy of the country.

United States: From Local Traditions to Global Phenomenon

The United States, the birthplace of the modern Valentine's Day celebration, has witnessed the transformation of local traditions into a global phenomenon. The exchange of cards, chocolates, and flowers, once rooted in local customs, has become universal symbols of love. The United States has played a central role in shaping the global celebration, and in turn, the celebration has influenced and transformed local expressions of love within the country.

Conclusion: Transformative Power of Love's Global Journey

As we explore how different cultures embrace and transform Western traditions, a common thread emerges – the transformative power of love's global journey. From Japan to

Brazil, South Korea to Egypt, the celebration of love reflects a dynamic interplay between global influences and local adaptations. Western traditions, once rooted in specific cultural contexts, have become part of a global tapestry of love, transformed and enriched by the diverse cultures they encounter. In the chapters that follow, we will continue to unravel the intricacies of love's expression, exploring global icons, enduring symbols, and the controversies that arise when love encounters societal norms. Join us as we navigate the transformative journey of love across borders, appreciating the beauty and diversity that define the celebration of love around the world.

Fusion of Local and Global Love Symbols

The celebration of love on Valentine's Day transcends geographical boundaries, intertwining local symbols with global influences. In this chapter, we explore how different cultures have fused their unique symbols with the global icons of love, creating a rich tapestry that reflects the intersection of the local and the universal.

Japan: Origami and Cherry Blossoms

In Japan, the celebration of love intertwines global symbols with local traditions. While the exchange of chocolates is a Western import, the presentation often involves intricate origami, adding a distinctly Japanese touch. Cherry blossoms, with their ephemeral beauty, become a symbol of transient love, blending seamlessly with the global icons of hearts and roses. The fusion of local craftsmanship with global symbols reflects Japan's ability to infuse cultural richness into the celebration of love.

India: Lotus and Mehndi Art

India's celebration of love incorporates global symbols while retaining its cultural identity. The lotus, a sacred flower in Hinduism, symbolizes purity and beauty and is often used to express love. Mehndi art, intricate henna designs applied to the hands, becomes a unique way to celebrate love, adding an indigenous flair to the global celebration. The fusion of lotus motifs and Mehndi art with traditional Western symbols illustrates how India seamlessly incorporates its cultural heritage into the global narrative of love.

Italy: Romantic Venues and Olive Trees

Italy, known for its romantic ambiance, infuses global symbols with local charm. While red roses and heart-shaped chocolates are universal, Italy enhances the celebration by incorporating its iconic romantic venues. The canals of Venice, the rolling hills of Tuscany, and the historic architecture become integral to the expression of love. Olive trees, with their cultural significance, add a local touch to the global celebration, creating a fusion that captures the essence of Italian romance.

South Korea: Locks of Love and K-Drama Inspirations

In South Korea, the celebration of love takes inspiration from global symbols while incorporating local traditions. "Locks of Love" bridges, adorned with padlocks symbolizing eternal love, have become popular. This practice, influenced by global trends, coexists with local symbols like the traditional hanbok. Additionally, South Korea's vibrant K-Drama culture influences romantic expressions, fusing globalized notions of love with local narratives.

Brazil: Copacabana Beach and Carnival Spirit

Brazil's celebration of love integrates global symbols with the vibrancy of its local culture. While red roses and heart-shaped chocolates are exchanged, the celebration often spills onto iconic locations like Copacabana Beach. The spirited atmosphere of Carnival, with its lively music and dance, becomes a backdrop for romantic expressions. This fusion of global symbols with the festive spirit of Brazil showcases the country's ability to infuse joy and energy into the celebration of love.

France: Eiffel Tower and French Elegance

In France, the celebration of love is inseparable from iconic landmarks like the Eiffel Tower. While global symbols like red roses and heart-shaped chocolates are exchanged, the French elevate the celebration with their inherent sense of elegance. The exchange of love letters, appreciation for fine arts, and the emphasis on romantic gestures add a layer of sophistication to the global celebration. France's fusion of global icons with its cultural refinement creates a celebration that is both timeless and uniquely French.

China: Double Happiness and Red Lanterns

China's celebration of love combines global symbols with traditional elements. While the exchange of red roses aligns with Western traditions, the symbol of "Double Happiness" holds cultural significance. Red lanterns, associated with festivals and celebrations, add a festive touch to the global celebration of love. The fusion of global symbols with traditional elements reflects China's ability to balance cultural heritage with contemporary expressions of affection.

Mexico: Papel Picado and Aztec Symbols

In Mexico, the celebration of love intertwines global symbols with indigenous traditions. Papel Picado, intricately cut paper banners, often featuring hearts and romantic motifs, become a local expression of love. Aztec symbols, such as the intertwined serpent, add an ancient touch to modern celebrations. The fusion of indigenous artistry with global symbols showcases Mexico's rich cultural tapestry in the expression of love.

United States: Hollywood Romance and Iconic Settings

The United States, as a cultural influencer, shapes the global celebration of love with its own symbols. Hollywood romance, epitomized in romantic movies, influences the global perception of love. Iconic settings like New York's Central Park or San Francisco's Golden Gate Bridge become integral to the global narrative. The fusion of Hollywood ideals with these iconic locations creates a celebration that reflects the U.S.'s cultural imprint on the global expression of love.

Middle East: Calligraphy and Symbolic Colors

In the Middle East, the celebration of love blends global symbols with regional art forms. Arabic calligraphy, often used to express romantic sentiments, adds a distinctive touch. Symbolic colors like gold and red, resonating with cultural meanings, become integral to the celebration. The fusion of calligraphy and symbolic colors with global symbols illustrates how the Middle East infuses its cultural richness into the global celebration of love.

Australia: Indigenous Art and Outdoor Celebrations

Australia's celebration of love integrates global symbols with its unique landscape and indigenous culture. While the exchange of cards and gifts aligns with Western traditions, the celebration often spills into the outdoors, embracing the country's natural beauty. Indigenous art, with its vibrant colors and storytelling, becomes a local expression of love. The fusion of global symbols with outdoor celebrations and indigenous art reflects Australia's ability to incorporate its diverse cultural elements into the global narrative of love.

Conclusion: Harmonizing Global and Local Harmonies

As we explore the fusion of local and global love symbols, a harmonious tapestry emerges. Different cultures contribute their unique colors and patterns to the celebration of love, creating a global narrative that resonates with local nuances. The fusion of symbols from around the world with indigenous elements showcases the adaptability and creativity of societies in expressing the universal emotion of love. In the chapters that follow, we will continue to unravel the intricate layers of love's expression, exploring global icons, enduring symbols, and the controversies that arise when love encounters societal norms. Join us as we navigate the harmonious interplay of global and local harmonies in the celebration of love around the world.

Chapter 3: Global Icons of Love and Romance
International Symbols in the Language of Love

In the universal language of love, symbols serve as powerful messengers, transcending cultural boundaries and expressing emotions that words may fail to capture. This chapter delves into the global icons that have become synonymous with love and romance, exploring how these symbols have traversed the world, acquiring diverse meanings and cultural adaptations along the way.

Hearts: Universality in Symbolism

At the heart of the global language of love lies the symbol of the heart itself. Universally recognized, the heart has become an iconic representation of affection, passion, and romantic attachment. Its simplicity and symmetry make it a versatile symbol, easily incorporated into various cultural expressions. Whether exchanged on a card in the West, drawn on the sands of a beach in the East, or created through intricate patterns in indigenous art, the heart symbolizes the universality of love that transcends borders.

Red Roses: Blossoming Expressions of Love

The red rose, with its velvety petals and rich color, has evolved into a global symbol of love and romance. Originating from Western traditions, where red roses were associated with the goddess of love, Venus, this iconic flower has crossed continents and cultural landscapes. In Asia, the symbolism of the red rose harmonizes with local expressions, while in the

Middle East, where red is associated with deep emotions, the rose becomes a potent symbol of passion. The red rose's journey across the world exemplifies how a flower can carry profound meanings in the language of love.

Cupid: Cross-Cultural Archery of Affection

Cupid, the mischievous winged deity of love in Western mythology, has transcended cultural boundaries to become a cross-cultural icon. His arrow, said to cause uncontrollable affection, resonates with the romantic aspirations of people globally. In various cultures, Cupid's image has been embraced and adapted, weaving into local narratives. From Japan's cherubic representations to South Korea's playful Cupid depictions, this winged messenger symbolizes the whimsical nature of love that transcends cultural differences.

Love Locks: Securing Affection Around the World

The tradition of attaching padlocks to bridges, known as Love Locks, has become a global phenomenon symbolizing eternal love. Originating in Europe, particularly in Paris, the practice has spread to iconic locations worldwide. Couples in Seoul, Moscow, and even as far as Australia now express their enduring love by attaching locks to bridges and tossing the keys into the water below. The universality of this practice illustrates how a simple act can become a global symbol of commitment and lasting affection.

Infinity Symbol: Eternal Connections

The infinity symbol, resembling a figure-eight on its side, has gained popularity as a representation of eternal love and connection. Originating in mathematics, the symbol found its way into the language of love, symbolizing an unending, limitless bond. Embraced globally, the infinity symbol is incorporated into jewelry, tattoos, and art, becoming a visual expression of enduring love that transcends cultural and linguistic barriers.

Mandalas: Spiritual Harmony in Love

The mandala, a geometric figure representing the universe in Hindu and Buddhist traditions, has become a symbol of spiritual unity and harmony in love. Its intricate patterns and circular design often incorporate symbols of love, and the act of creating or sharing mandalas becomes a meditative expression of affection. From India to the United States, the mandala's representation of interconnectedness resonates with those seeking a spiritual dimension in their romantic connections.

Swans: Graceful Partnerships

Swans, known for their lifelong monogamous partnerships, have become a symbol of enduring love and fidelity. This graceful bird's representation of devotion has transcended cultural boundaries, finding a place in various global expressions of love. From European folklore to Asian symbolism, the swan's elegance and commitment serve as a metaphor for the timeless and faithful nature of true love.

Eternal Knots: Cultural Weaving of Love

In various cultures, the symbol of the eternal knot represents unbreakable connections and interdependence. Originating in Buddhist traditions, particularly in Tibetan culture, the eternal knot has found its way into global expressions of love. Whether integrated into jewelry or as standalone symbols, the eternal knot signifies the timeless nature of love and the interconnectedness of individuals. Its cross-cultural adoption exemplifies how certain symbols can resonate universally in the celebration of love.

Promise Rings: Global Tokens of Commitment

The tradition of exchanging promise rings, a symbol of commitment and future engagement, has become a global practice. Originating in Western cultures, this gesture has spread to various parts of the world, symbolizing a mutual promise of love and dedication. The act of giving and receiving promise rings transcends cultural differences, embodying the universal desire for lasting commitments in romantic relationships.

Moon and Stars: Celestial Connections

The moon and stars, with their celestial beauty, have become symbols of everlasting connections and romantic aspirations. Across cultures, from ancient myths to contemporary expressions of love, these celestial bodies evoke a sense of timelessness and cosmic unity. Whether portrayed in poetry, art, or jewelry, the moon and stars serve as enduring symbols that capture the transcendent nature of love in the vast expanse of the universe.

Music Notes: Harmonizing Hearts

The language of love extends to the realm of music, where notes and melodies become symbolic expressions of affection. Across cultures, the act of sharing music or dedicating songs to loved ones transcends linguistic barriers. Whether through classical compositions, folk tunes, or modern pop songs, music notes serve as a harmonizing force that connects hearts globally, illustrating the ability of sound to convey the emotions of love.

Conclusion: Love's Global Lexicon

As we explore the international symbols in the language of love, a global lexicon emerges—a collection of visual expressions that convey the timeless and universal emotions of affection and romance. These symbols, ranging from hearts to roses, Cupid to love locks, bridge cultural divides, serving as a common vocabulary for expressing the complexities and beauty of love. In the chapters that follow, we will continue to unravel the intricate layers of love's expression, exploring enduring symbols, global controversies, and the historical perspectives that shape the celebration of love around the world. Join us as we navigate the rich tapestry of love's global lexicon, appreciating the diversity and unity that these symbols bring to the universal language of love.

Shared Cultural References in Global Romanticism

Love is a language that transcends borders, and in the realm of global romanticism, shared cultural references become threads that weave diverse societies into a tapestry of universal affection. This chapter explores how certain cultural references, whether rooted in mythology, literature, or art, have become touchstones of love across the world, shaping a shared understanding of romance that traverses cultural boundaries.

Romeo and Juliet: Tragic Romance as a Global Archetype

The tale of Romeo and Juliet, Shakespeare's iconic tragedy of star-crossed lovers, has permeated cultures worldwide, becoming a shared cultural reference in global romanticism. The themes of forbidden love, societal opposition, and tragic sacrifice resonate universally, transcending linguistic and cultural differences. From adaptations in Bollywood to references in K-Dramas, the enduring legacy of Romeo and Juliet illustrates how this timeless narrative has become a touchstone for expressions of romantic longing and societal challenges in love.

Laila Majnu: Middle Eastern Echoes of Forbidden Love

In the Middle East, the story of Laila Majnu echoes the tragic theme of forbidden love. Rooted in Persian and Arabic literature, this tale of an ill-fated romance has become a shared cultural reference that transcends regional and linguistic boundaries. Variations of the story are found in literature, music, and film across the Middle East and South Asia, creating a narrative that symbolizes the intensity and challenges of love that resonate globally.

Butterfly Lovers: Chinese Parallel to Romeo and Juliet

China's Butterfly Lovers, also known as the Chinese Romeo and Juliet, is a classical love story that dates back to ancient times. The narrative of a forbidden romance between a young woman disguised as a man and her male counterpart has become a shared cultural reference in Chinese romanticism. This tale of enduring love has inspired numerous adaptations in literature, opera, and film, creating a cultural touchstone that captures the essence of universal romantic themes.

Tristan and Iseult: Celtic Romance Across Continents

The Celtic legend of Tristan and Iseult, a tale of love, betrayal, and tragedy, has transcended its European origins to become a global reference in romantic literature. Adaptations and references to this ancient story are found in literature, art, and even modern popular culture. The enduring appeal of Tristan and Iseult lies in its exploration of love's complexities and the eternal quest for a transcendent, transformative connection.

Heer Ranjha: South Asian Cultural Gem of Enduring Love

In South Asia, the tale of Heer Ranjha, a Punjabi folktale of tragic love, has become a cultural gem that resonates across the region. The story, rooted in Punjabi Sufi poetry, explores the challenges of societal norms and the power of love to overcome adversity. Adaptations of Heer Ranjha in literature, theater, and film showcase its enduring appeal as a shared cultural reference in South Asian romanticism.

The Lady and the Unicorn: Symbolic Love in Medieval Art

The Lady and the Unicorn, a series of medieval tapestries from France, has become a symbolic representation of courtly love and romance. The tapestries, featuring a mysterious lady surrounded by unicorns and other mythical creatures, convey the ideals of chivalry and romantic longing. Despite originating in medieval Europe, the symbolism of The Lady and the Unicorn has found resonance in global art and literature, symbolizing the universal themes of love, purity, and mystery.

Majnun Layla: Arabic Poetic Expression of Devotion

The Arabic legend of Majnun Layla, a tale of passionate and unrequited love, has left an indelible mark on the region's cultural landscape. Originating from pre-Islamic Arabic poetry, the story has inspired countless artistic interpretations, including literature, music, and visual arts. Majnun Layla's enduring presence in Middle Eastern culture highlights its role as a shared cultural reference, expressing the timeless theme of profound and transformative love.

Taj Mahal: Monumental Symbol of Love

The Taj Mahal, a white marble mausoleum in India, stands as a monumental symbol of love and devotion. Built by the Mughal emperor Shah Jahan in memory of his wife Mumtaz Mahal, this architectural marvel has become a global reference for romantic grandeur. Its influence is evident in various global cultural expressions, as artists, writers, and filmmakers draw inspiration from the Taj Mahal as a representation of eternal love.

Cinderella: Fairy Tale Romance Transcending Cultures

The Cinderella story, with its themes of transformation, love, and the search for a soulmate, transcends cultural and regional boundaries. Variations of the Cinderella narrative are found in folktales and literature across the world, each adaptation infusing local elements while retaining the core romantic themes. From European fairy tales to Asian folklore, Cinderella's journey from rags to riches symbolizes the universal dream of love's transformative power.

Yun Jin: Korean Symbol of Enduring Affection

In Korean culture, the image of Yun Jin, a pair of intertwined swans, has become a symbol of enduring affection and fidelity. Derived from a Korean folktale, this symbol represents the idea of eternal love and marital harmony. Yun Jin's presence in Korean art, jewelry, and cultural expressions illustrates its role as a shared reference that conveys the ideals of lasting love and devotion.

Conclusion: Love's Cultural Harmony

As we explore shared cultural references in global romanticism, a harmonious blend of narratives, symbols, and archetypes emerges—a testament to the universality of love. Whether rooted in ancient mythology, medieval art, or timeless folktales, these cultural touchstones resonate across borders, connecting societies in a shared understanding of the complexities and beauty of romantic relationships. In the chapters that follow, we will continue to unravel the intricate layers of love's expression, exploring enduring symbols, global controversies, and historical perspectives that shape the celebration of love around the world. Join us as we navigate the cultural harmony that underlies the global language of love.

Icons Crossing Cultural Barriers

In the rich tapestry of global romanticism, certain icons have demonstrated an extraordinary ability to traverse cultural barriers. These symbols, whether rooted in mythology, literature, or art, have transcended their cultural origins, becoming universally recognized expressions of love. This chapter explores the stories and symbols that have successfully crossed borders, enriching the global language of love with their enduring presence.

Heart-Shaped Hands: Gestures of Love Beyond Words

The heart-shaped hands gesture, formed by intertwining the fingers to create a heart shape, has become a universal symbol of love and affection. Originating in Western cultures, this simple yet powerful gesture has crossed cultural barriers to become a global expression of heartfelt emotions. From Asia to Africa, people around the world use this hand symbol to convey love, transcending linguistic differences and embodying a shared understanding of the universal language of affection.

Red Roses: A Global Bouquet of Love

The red rose, deeply rooted in Western symbolism, has blossomed into a global icon of love. Its velvety petals and rich color evoke passion and romance, transcending cultural differences. From Europe to Asia, the exchange of red roses has become a cross-cultural expression of affection. The global appeal of this iconic flower lies in its ability to convey deep emotions, making it a symbol that resonates across continents.

Cupid: Wings of Love Beyond Cultural Boundaries

Cupid, the mischievous winged deity of love in Western mythology, has transcended cultural boundaries to become a global symbol of romantic aspirations. His arrow, said to cause uncontrollable affection, resonates with the universal desire for love and connection. From Europe to Asia, Cupid's image has been embraced and adapted, illustrating how the wings of love can span continents and cultures.

Infinity Symbol: Limitless Love Recognized Worldwide

The infinity symbol, resembling a figure-eight on its side, has become a global icon representing eternal love and connection. Originating in mathematical concepts, the symbol's interpretation shifted to embody unending affection. Embraced across cultures, the infinity symbol is now recognized worldwide as a representation of enduring love that transcends cultural and linguistic boundaries.

Love Locks: Securing Affection Universally

The tradition of attaching padlocks to bridges, known as Love Locks, has become a global phenomenon symbolizing everlasting love. Originating in Europe, particularly in Paris, the practice has spread to iconic locations worldwide. Couples from Asia to the Americas express their commitment by attaching locks to bridges, creating a global symbol of enduring affection that transcends cultural and geographical distances.

Moon and Stars: Celestial Icons in Global Skies

The moon and stars, with their celestial beauty, have become symbols of everlasting connections and romantic aspirations across cultures. From ancient myths to contemporary expressions of love, these celestial bodies transcend cultural differences. Whether portrayed in poetry, art, or jewelry, the moon and stars serve as enduring symbols that capture the transcendent nature of love in the vast expanse of the global universe.

Music Notes: Harmonizing Hearts Globally

The language of love extends to the realm of music, where notes and melodies become symbolic expressions of affection. Across cultures, from classical compositions to modern pop songs, music notes serve as a harmonizing force that connects hearts globally. The ability of sound to convey the emotions of love transcends linguistic barriers, creating a shared cultural experience that resonates universally.

Promise Rings: Global Tokens of Commitment

The tradition of exchanging promise rings, symbolizing commitment and future engagement, has become a global practice. Originating in Western cultures, this gesture has spread to various parts of the world, symbolizing a mutual promise of love and dedication. The act of giving and receiving promise rings transcends cultural differences, embodying the universal desire for lasting commitments in romantic relationships.

Eiffel Tower: A Global Monument to Romance

The Eiffel Tower, an iconic landmark in Paris, has become a global symbol of romance and love. While rooted in Western history and culture, the Eiffel Tower's image is embraced worldwide as an emblem of romantic grandeur. From Asia to the Americas, the silhouette of this Parisian monument evokes a sense of timeless love that transcends cultural and geographical boundaries.

Soulmate Symbols: Universal Quest for Connection

Symbols representing soulmates, whether depicted as two halves of a heart, entwined vines, or interlocking puzzle pieces, have become universally recognized icons of the quest for connection. This transcultural symbol embodies the desire to find a kindred spirit, and its presence in various forms across cultures reflects the shared human longing for profound and meaningful connections.

Swans: Graceful Partnerships Worldwide

Swans, known for their lifelong monogamous partnerships, have become a symbol of enduring love and fidelity recognized globally. This graceful bird's representation of devotion transcends cultural boundaries, resonating with diverse societies. From European folklore to Asian symbolism, the swan's elegance and commitment serve as a metaphor for the timeless and faithful nature of true love.

Taj Mahal: Cross-Cultural Monument of Love

The Taj Mahal, a white marble mausoleum in India, stands as a cross-cultural symbol of love and devotion. Built by the Mughal emperor Shah Jahan in memory of his wife Mumtaz Mahal, this architectural marvel has become a global reference for romantic grandeur. Its influence is evident in various cultural expressions, as artists, writers, and filmmakers draw inspiration from the Taj Mahal as a representation of eternal love.

Conclusion: Icons Uniting Hearts Worldwide

As we explore icons crossing cultural barriers in the global language of love, a common theme emerges—the ability of certain symbols to unite hearts worldwide. From the infinity symbol to the Eiffel Tower, these icons transcend cultural and geographical differences, embodying the shared human experience of love. In the chapters that follow, we will continue to unravel the intricate layers of love's expression, exploring enduring symbols, global controversies, and historical perspectives that shape the celebration of love around the world. Join us as we navigate the universal language of love, where iconic symbols become bridges connecting hearts across diverse cultures.

Enduring Global Symbols of Love

Love, as a universal language, finds expression through enduring symbols that stand the test of time. In this chapter, we explore the timeless icons that have become entrenched in the global celebration of love, transcending cultural and geographical boundaries. These symbols, whether rooted in mythology, art, or tradition, continue to resonate across generations, embodying the enduring nature of love in the collective human experience.

Wedding Rings: Circles of Commitment

The exchange of wedding rings is a global tradition that symbolizes the eternal nature of love and commitment. The circular shape of the ring represents an unending bond between partners, regardless of cultural differences. From ancient cultures to modern societies, the act of exchanging rings during marriage ceremonies is a universal practice that signifies the timeless commitment two individuals make to each other.

Red Roses: Blooms of Passion

The red rose, with its vibrant color and velvety petals, has transcended cultural boundaries to become a global symbol of love and passion. Universally recognized, the red rose conveys deep emotions and romantic feelings. From Western traditions to Eastern celebrations, the exchange of red roses is a timeless gesture that signifies affection, making it one of the most enduring symbols of love across the world.

Heart Symbol: Universality in Affection

The heart symbol, a simple yet powerful representation of love, is universally recognized across cultures. Whether drawn on a Valentine's Day card in Western countries or incorporated into traditional art in the East, the heart symbolizes affection and emotional connection. Its simplicity and universality make it an enduring icon that transcends cultural and linguistic differences, becoming a visual expression of love understood by people worldwide.

Cupid: Arrow of Romantic Aspirations

Cupid, the cherubic deity of love in Western mythology, has become an enduring symbol of romantic aspirations. Armed with his bow and arrow, Cupid represents the whimsical and unpredictable nature of love. The image of Cupid has permeated cultures around the world, with various adaptations and representations, making it a cross-cultural icon that embodies the universal desire for affection and connection.

Love Locks: Eternal Bonds in Metal

Love Locks, the practice of attaching padlocks to bridges and other landmarks, has become a global symbol of enduring love. Originating in Europe, this tradition has spread to cities worldwide, symbolizing the unbreakable bond between couples. The act of securing a lock and tossing away the key has become a shared ritual that transcends cultural and geographical boundaries, turning bridges into tangible expressions of lasting affection.

Moon and Stars: Celestial Harmony in Love

The moon and stars, with their celestial beauty, have been embraced as symbols of love across cultures and centuries. Whether depicted in ancient poetry, traditional art, or modern expressions, these celestial bodies evoke a sense of eternal connection and cosmic unity. The enduring symbolism of the moon and stars reflects the universal human aspiration for enduring love that reaches beyond the confines of earthly existence.

Swans: Graceful Partnerships Across Continents

Swans, known for their lifelong monogamous partnerships, have become a cross-cultural symbol of enduring love. From European folklore to Asian symbolism, the elegant swan embodies the qualities of commitment, fidelity, and grace in romantic relationships. The swan's representation of enduring partnerships resonates globally, illustrating the timeless and faithful nature of true love.

Eternal Knot: Cultural Threads of Love

The Eternal Knot, a symbol often associated with Buddhism and Celtic traditions, represents unbreakable connections and interdependence. Found in jewelry, art, and ceremonial objects, the Eternal Knot transcends cultural boundaries, becoming a global symbol of everlasting love. Its intricate design and universal significance make it an enduring icon that speaks to the interconnectedness of individuals in the journey of love.

Taj Mahal: Architectural Marvel of Devotion

The Taj Mahal, a white marble mausoleum in India, stands as an enduring architectural symbol of love. Built by Emperor Shah Jahan in memory of his wife Mumtaz Mahal, this iconic structure has captured the world's imagination as a testament to the power of love. The Taj Mahal's influence extends beyond its cultural origins, becoming a global representation of grandeur, devotion, and eternal love.

Promise Rings: Vows of Future Commitment

Promise rings, exchanged as tokens of commitment and future engagement, have become a global symbol of enduring love. Originating in Western cultures, the act of giving and receiving promise rings has spread to various parts of the world, symbolizing a mutual promise of love and dedication. The universal desire for lasting commitments in romantic relationships is embodied in the act of exchanging promise rings.

Butterfly Symbol: Metamorphosis of Love

The butterfly, with its transformative journey from caterpillar to winged beauty, has become a global symbol of metamorphosis in love. Across cultures, the butterfly is associated with change, growth, and the beauty that emerges from transformation. Whether depicted in art, literature, or as a personal symbol, the butterfly transcends cultural boundaries, representing the universal theme of evolving love.

Eiffel Tower: Parisian Emblem of Romance

The Eiffel Tower, an iconic landmark in Paris, has become a global emblem of romance. While rooted in Western history and culture, the Eiffel Tower's image is embraced worldwide as a representation of romantic grandeur. From Asia to the Americas, the silhouette of this Parisian monument evokes a sense of timeless love that transcends cultural and geographical boundaries.

Conclusion: Symbols Beyond Borders

As we explore enduring global symbols of love, a common thread emerges—the ability of certain icons to transcend cultural and geographical borders, weaving into the fabric of the global celebration of love. From wedding rings to the Taj Mahal, these symbols embody the universal nature of affection, connecting people across diverse cultures and societies. In the chapters that follow, we will continue to unravel the intricate layers of love's expression, exploring global controversies, historical perspectives, and the impact of modern trends on the celebration of love worldwide. Join us as we navigate the timeless symbols that bind hearts beyond borders, creating a shared language of love that resonates across the world.

Chapter 4: Controversies and Criticisms Worldwide Cultural Debates on Valentine's Day Observance

While Valentine's Day is widely celebrated as a day of love and affection, its observance has not been without controversy. Cultural debates surrounding the traditions and practices associated with Valentine's Day have emerged worldwide, reflecting diverse perspectives on love, romance, and the influence of Western customs. In this chapter, we delve into the cultural debates that surround the observance of Valentine's Day, exploring both the criticisms and the defenders of this global celebration.

Origins and Evolution: Unpacking Valentine's Day Debates

The debates surrounding Valentine's Day often begin with a consideration of its origins and how it has evolved over time. Critics argue that the modern celebration of Valentine's Day, characterized by the exchange of gifts, cards, and romantic gestures, has strayed far from its historical roots. Supporters, on the other hand, contend that the essence of expressing love and affection remains at the heart of the celebration, irrespective of its commercialized aspects.

Cultural Appropriation: Western Influence on Global Celebrations

One prominent debate centers around the accusation of cultural appropriation, asserting that the widespread adoption of Western Valentine's Day customs infringes on local traditions and values. Critics argue that the commercialization of love, as promoted by Western media and businesses, has eroded indigenous expressions of affection. Defenders counter that cultural exchange is a natural part of globalization, and the blending of traditions enriches the diversity of Valentine's Day celebrations.

Religious Perspectives: Clash with Traditional Values

In certain religious circles, the observance of Valentine's Day is met with skepticism and criticism. Some argue that the origins of the holiday, often associated with Christian martyrs named Valentine, clash with religious principles. This debate extends beyond Christianity, with objections raised by adherents of various faiths who question the compatibility of Valentine's Day with their religious values.

Commercialization of Love: Critiques on Consumerism

A pervasive criticism of Valentine's Day revolves around its commercialization. Detractors argue that the holiday has been exploited by businesses to boost sales through the promotion of gifts, cards, and extravagant gestures. Critics question the sincerity of expressions of love when they are tied to consumerist practices. Supporters counter that thoughtful gestures and genuine expressions of affection can coexist with commercial elements, emphasizing the personal meaning behind the celebrations.

Gender Dynamics: Pressures and Expectations

The gendered aspects of Valentine's Day have sparked discussions on societal expectations and pressures. Critics argue that the holiday reinforces traditional gender roles and places undue pressure on individuals to conform to romantic stereotypes. The expectation for men to be the primary gift-givers and women to be recipients has been challenged, with advocates for more inclusive and egalitarian expressions of love.

Singles Awareness: Inclusivity and Empowerment

A counter-narrative has emerged in the form of Singles Awareness Day (SAD), challenging the perceived exclusivity of Valentine's Day. Advocates argue that the emphasis on romantic relationships can be alienating for those who are single or uninterested in traditional expressions of love. Singles Awareness Day aims to promote self-love, friendship, and a broader understanding of diverse forms of affection.

Cultural Resistance: Reinforcing Identity

In certain cultures, resistance to Valentine's Day is rooted in a desire to preserve and reinforce local traditions. Some argue that the imposition of Western customs diminishes the richness of indigenous expressions of love. Cultural resistance manifests in various forms, from alternative celebrations to outright rejection of Valentine's Day as a foreign import.

Globalization and Homogenization: Loss of Diversity

The global spread of Valentine's Day has led to concerns about the homogenization of love expressions. Critics contend that as the holiday becomes more standardized worldwide, unique cultural variations in expressing affection are being overshadowed. Supporters, however, argue that the global celebration allows for the exchange of diverse love traditions, fostering cross-cultural understanding.

Alternative Celebrations: Rethinking Love Traditions

In response to the controversies surrounding Valentine's Day, some communities have developed alternative celebrations that align more closely with their cultural values. These alternatives often emphasize community, familial, or platonic love rather than romantic partnerships. Advocates argue that embracing alternative celebrations fosters inclusivity and allows for a more authentic expression of affection.

Governmental Interventions: Banning or Regulating Celebrations

In certain regions, governmental authorities have intervened in Valentine's Day celebrations. In some cases, the holiday has been banned outright due to religious or cultural objections. In other instances, regulations have been imposed to control the scale and nature of observances. This debate raises questions about the role of the state in shaping cultural practices and expressions of love.

Conclusion: Navigating Diverse Perspectives

As we navigate the cultural debates on Valentine's Day observance, it becomes evident that diverse perspectives shape the understanding and celebration of love worldwide. From critiques of commercialization to concerns about cultural appropriation, the debates surrounding Valentine's Day reflect the complexities of navigating global traditions. In the chapters that follow, we will continue to explore the impact of love on a global scale, examining historical perspectives, enduring symbols, and modern trends that contribute to the rich tapestry of love celebrations across borders. Join us as we delve deeper into the intricacies of love's expression and the controversies that arise in its global celebration.

Resisting and Reinterpreting Western Influences

The globalization of Valentine's Day has brought with it a myriad of cultural debates, and one prominent discourse centers on the resistance to and reinterpretation of Western influences on love celebrations. From critiques of cultural imperialism to efforts to infuse local traditions with new meanings, this chapter explores how various societies around the world grapple with the impact of Western-centric expressions of love, challenging, adapting, and reclaiming Valentine's Day in unique ways.

Cultural Imperialism and Love: The Challenge of Westernization

Critics argue that the global celebration of Valentine's Day is emblematic of cultural imperialism, asserting that Western values and practices dominate and marginalize local expressions of affection. The charge is that the commercialized version of love promoted by Western media and businesses overshadows indigenous traditions, prompting resistance from those who seek to protect and preserve their cultural identity in the face of perceived Westernization.

Local Traditions Under Siege: Balancing Act in the Face of Globalization

As Valentine's Day gains global prominence, there is a growing concern that local love traditions are under siege. Some societies resist the encroachment of Western customs, viewing them as a threat to cultural authenticity. This resistance is not merely about rejecting external influences but involves a delicate balancing act—preserving cherished local practices while navigating the realities of an interconnected world.

Adapting Indigenous Expressions: The Evolution of Love Celebrations

Rather than outright rejection, some cultures choose to adapt and integrate Western Valentine's Day customs into their existing love celebrations. This adaptation often involves a process of reinterpretation, where imported practices are given new meanings rooted in local cultural contexts. This approach seeks to reconcile global influences with the need to maintain cultural distinctiveness, leading to the emergence of hybrid celebrations.

Fusion of East and West: Creating a Synthesized Celebration

In some regions, a synthesis of Eastern and Western elements has given rise to unique love celebrations that capture the essence of both traditions. This fusion represents an intentional blending of diverse cultural influences, acknowledging the global nature of love while incorporating indigenous symbols and practices. The result is a celebration that reflects a harmonious coexistence of East and West in the realm of romantic expressions.

National Pride and Cultural Identity: A Call for Preservation

The resistance to Western influences on Valentine's Day is often intertwined with a broader sense of national pride and the preservation of cultural identity. Defenders argue that safeguarding indigenous expressions of love is essential for maintaining the unique fabric of their societies. In this context, the critique of Valentine's Day becomes a rallying point for cultural preservation, emphasizing the importance of love celebrations rooted in local values.

Community-Based Alternatives: Strengthening Ties Locally

Some communities respond to the influence of Western love traditions by fostering alternative celebrations rooted in communal bonds. These initiatives prioritize local connections, emphasizing the importance of familial, platonic, and community-based affections. By redirecting the focus away from romantic partnerships, these alternatives aim to strengthen social ties within the community while resisting external pressures to conform to Western norms.

Educational Initiatives: Shaping Cultural Narratives

Efforts to resist and reinterpret Western influences often extend to educational initiatives aimed at shaping cultural narratives surrounding love celebrations. Schools and cultural institutions may play a role in promoting awareness of local traditions, fostering critical thinking about the impact of globalization on love practices, and empowering individuals to make informed choices about how they express affection.

Media and Representation: Redefining the Narrative

Media, as a powerful influencer of cultural narratives, becomes a battleground for the resistance and reinterpretation of Western influences. Some regions take deliberate steps to reshape media portrayals of love, presenting alternative narratives that reflect local values and traditions. This includes promoting diverse representations of affection that go beyond the stereotypical Western expressions often depicted in mainstream media.

Legal and Policy Interventions: Protecting Cultural Heritage

In certain cases, governments may implement legal and policy interventions to protect and preserve cultural heritage in the face of Westernization. This can involve measures to regulate the commercialization of Valentine's Day, restrict certain practices, or promote alternative celebrations that align more closely with local values. These interventions reflect a broader commitment to safeguarding cultural identity in the realm of love expressions.

Global Awareness Movements: Building Solidarity Across Borders

Resistance to Western influences on love celebrations is not confined to specific regions but can become a global awareness movement. Individuals and organizations advocating for cultural diversity and the preservation of indigenous expressions of love form networks that build solidarity across borders. This movement seeks to create a collective consciousness that values the richness of global cultural diversity in the celebration of love.

Conclusion: Navigating Cultural Crossroads

The resistance to and reinterpretation of Western influences on love celebrations reflect the complex interplay between globalization and cultural identity. From outright rejection to the synthesis of East and West, cultures navigate the crossroads of tradition and modernity, seeking to define and express love in ways that resonate with their unique cultural narratives. In the chapters that follow, we will continue to explore the controversies and criticisms surrounding the global celebration of love, examining historical perspectives, enduring symbols, and modern trends that shape the diverse tapestry of love expressions worldwide. Join us as we delve deeper into the intricate dance between tradition and transformation in the realm of love celebrations across borders.

Critiques on the Commercialization of Love

As Valentine's Day has evolved into a global celebration of love, it has not escaped criticism, particularly in the realm of commercialization. Critics argue that the holiday, once rooted in expressions of affection, has been increasingly influenced by consumerism and materialism. This chapter delves into the critiques on the commercialization of love, exploring how the commodification of affection impacts the essence of Valentine's Day and sparks debates on authenticity, sincerity, and the true meaning of love.

The Evolution of Love into a Consumerist Celebration

Critics of the commercialization of love on Valentine's Day often point to the historical evolution of the holiday. What started as a day to express genuine affection through handwritten notes and simple gestures has transformed into a consumerist spectacle dominated by the exchange of gifts, cards, and elaborate romantic gestures. The transition from intimate expressions to commodified showcases of love raises questions about the sincerity and authenticity of contemporary celebrations.

The Gifting Culture: From Sentiment to Materialism

A primary focus of critiques revolves around the culture of gift-giving associated with Valentine's Day. Critics argue that the pressure to exchange elaborate and often expensive gifts has shifted the focus from the sentiment behind the gesture to the material value of the gifts. This transition, they contend, commodifies love, turning it into a transactional experience rather than a heartfelt expression of affection.

Influence of Mass Media: Crafting Expectations and Desires

Mass media plays a significant role in shaping societal expectations and desires surrounding Valentine's Day. Critics argue that the pervasive influence of advertisements, movies, and social media sets unrealistic standards for expressions of love. The portrayal of extravagant gestures and luxury gifts as the norm creates an atmosphere where the commercial aspects of the holiday overshadow the personal and intimate nature of genuine affection.

Consumerist Pressures on Relationships: Navigating Expectations

The commercialization of love on Valentine's Day can exert pressures on individuals and relationships. Critics contend that societal expectations, fueled by consumerist influences, create a sense of obligation to conform to certain standards of celebration. This pressure, they argue, can strain relationships and lead to feelings of inadequacy when individuals cannot meet the commercialized expectations associated with the holiday.

The Valentine's Day Industry: Profiting from Affection

The growth of a dedicated Valentine's Day industry, encompassing florists, chocolatiers, greeting card companies, and various retailers, has been a focal point of criticism. Critics argue that the commodification of love has turned Valentine's Day into a profit-driven enterprise, with businesses capitalizing on societal norms and expectations to boost sales. The commercialization, they contend, compromises the genuine and personal nature of expressions of affection.

Affordability and Inclusivity: Excluding Marginalized Groups

Critics also highlight issues of affordability and inclusivity in the commercialization of Valentine's Day. The emphasis on expensive gifts and grand gestures, they argue, excludes individuals and couples who may not have the financial means to participate in the consumerist aspects of the celebration. This exclusion, they contend, reinforces socioeconomic disparities and undermines the inclusivity of love expressions.

Pressure on Singles: Alienation and Stigmatization

The commercialization of love on Valentine's Day can contribute to the alienation and stigmatization of individuals who are not in romantic relationships. Critics argue that the pervasive focus on romantic partnerships marginalizes and stigmatizes single individuals. The pressure to conform to societal norms and participate in consumer-driven celebrations, they contend, can create feelings of loneliness and inadequacy among those not in romantic relationships.

Environmental Impact: Excessive Consumption and Waste

Another dimension of criticism centers around the environmental impact of the commercialization of Valentine's Day. The production and disposal of mass-produced cards, gifts, and decorations contribute to environmental degradation. Critics argue that the culture of disposable and often non-recyclable items associated with the holiday adds to the global issue of excessive consumption and waste.

Loss of Personal Touch: Authenticity in Jeopardy

Critics contend that the commercialization of love jeopardizes the authenticity and personal touch of expressions of affection. The emphasis on standardized gifts and gestures, they argue, diminishes the uniqueness of personal expressions of love. The commodification, they contend, erodes the intimate and thoughtful nature of genuine affection, replacing it with generic and mass-produced tokens of love.

Capitalizing on Emotional Vulnerability: Ethical Concerns

Critics also raise ethical concerns about businesses capitalizing on the emotional vulnerability associated with love. The commodification of affection, they argue, exploits individuals' desire for connection and intimacy, turning genuine emotions into marketable products. This critique questions the ethics of profiting from the emotional landscape of relationships.

Reclaiming the Essence of Valentine's Day: Alternative Approaches

In response to the critiques on the commercialization of love, there is a growing movement to reclaim the essence of Valentine's Day. Some individuals and communities advocate for alternative approaches that prioritize meaningful experiences, personal connections, and acts of kindness over consumerist practices. These alternatives seek to counterbalance the commercial aspects with a return to the heartfelt and authentic expressions of love.

Conclusion: Navigating the Commercial Landscape of Love

The critiques on the commercialization of love highlight the tension between the genuine expression of affection and the commodified aspects of Valentine's Day. As we navigate the commercial landscape of love, it becomes clear that the essence of the holiday is contested terrain, with debates centering on authenticity, inclusivity, and the impact of consumerism on relationships. In the chapters that follow, we will continue to explore the controversies and criticisms surrounding the global celebration of love, examining historical perspectives, enduring symbols, and modern trends that shape the diverse tapestry of love expressions worldwide. Join us as we delve deeper into the intricate dance between commerce and love in the realm of Valentine's Day celebrations across borders.

Balancing Global Trends with Cultural Identity

As Valentine's Day continues to traverse cultural boundaries, the question of how to balance global trends with cultural identity becomes a central theme. This chapter explores the challenges and strategies employed by diverse societies in reconciling the universal celebration of love with the preservation of cultural distinctiveness. From navigating the influence of Western traditions to embracing a global vision of love, cultures grapple with finding equilibrium in the face of evolving trends.

Embracing a Global Celebration of Love

While some societies resist external influences on Valentine's Day, others actively embrace the global celebration of love. Advocates for this approach argue that the universal nature of love provides an opportunity for cross-cultural understanding and shared experiences. Embracing a global celebration involves integrating diverse traditions and adopting certain elements of Valentine's Day while retaining local customs, creating a harmonious coexistence between the global and the indigenous.

Cultural Hybridity: Synthesizing Global and Local Elements

A common strategy in balancing global trends with cultural identity is the creation of cultural hybridity. This involves synthesizing global and local elements to form a unique expression of love that reflects both the influence of

Valentine's Day and the cultural values of a specific community. This approach allows for the preservation of identity while acknowledging the impact of global trends in shaping contemporary love celebrations.

Selective Adaptation: Incorporating Global Practices Thoughtfully

Some cultures opt for selective adaptation, choosing specific global practices that align with their values and traditions. This approach involves a thoughtful integration of elements from Valentine's Day that resonate with the local community. By carefully selecting and adapting certain customs, cultures can participate in the global celebration of love while maintaining a sense of cultural authenticity.

Educational Initiatives: Building Awareness and Understanding

Educational initiatives play a crucial role in fostering an understanding of global trends and their impact on cultural identity. By promoting awareness of the historical context of Valentine's Day and its evolution, societies can empower individuals to make informed choices about how they engage with the celebration. Education becomes a tool for navigating the complexities of global influences while preserving cultural distinctiveness.

Community Dialogues: Shaping Shared Values

Open and inclusive community dialogues provide spaces for individuals to discuss the impact of global trends on love celebrations. These discussions allow communities to collectively shape shared values and establish norms that strike a balance between the global and the local. Through dialogue, communities can navigate cultural nuances and collaboratively define the essence of their love traditions.

Cultural Festivals: Reinforcing Indigenous Expressions

Some cultures reinforce their indigenous expressions of love through the establishment of cultural festivals. These festivals serve as platforms for showcasing local traditions, art, and performances that highlight the unique ways in which love is celebrated within the community. By elevating and celebrating their own love customs, cultures assert their distinctiveness in the midst of global trends.

Governmental Support: Crafting Policies for Cultural Preservation

Governmental support is instrumental in crafting policies that balance global trends with cultural preservation. By acknowledging the importance of cultural identity, governments can implement measures to protect and promote indigenous expressions of love. This may include supporting local artisans, organizing cultural events, or integrating cultural education into public programs.

Creative Arts: Expressing Cultural Identity Through Artistic Endeavors

The creative arts serve as powerful mediums for expressing cultural identity. Through literature, music, visual arts, and performance, societies can convey the unique aspects of their love traditions. Creative endeavors become a means of both preserving cultural identity and participating in the global conversation on love, offering a nuanced and authentic representation of local customs.

Local Businesses: Fostering Cultural Sustainability

Local businesses play a vital role in balancing global trends with cultural identity. By supporting and promoting local artisans, businesses contribute to the sustainability of cultural practices. This approach encourages a shift away from mass-produced, globalized expressions of love, fostering an appreciation for locally crafted and culturally significant tokens of affection.

Digital Platforms: Global Connection with Local Roots

The use of digital platforms allows cultures to maintain global connections while preserving local roots. Social media, online forums, and digital storytelling become tools for sharing cultural narratives on love with a global audience. By leveraging technology, societies can engage in cross-cultural exchanges while reinforcing the importance of their own love traditions.

Cross-Generational Dialogue: Bridging Perspectives

Cross-generational dialogue is essential for navigating the tensions between global trends and cultural identity. By engaging in conversations that span different age groups, communities can bridge perspectives and find common ground. This dialogue fosters an understanding of the evolving nature of love celebrations and ensures that cultural identity remains relevant and meaningful across generations.

Conclusion: Crafting a Unique Tapestry of Love

Balancing global trends with cultural identity in the celebration of love is a nuanced and ongoing process. As cultures navigate the influences of Valentine's Day and other global practices, they craft unique tapestries that reflect the intricacies of their identity. In the chapters that follow, we will continue to explore the controversies and criticisms surrounding the global celebration of love, examining historical perspectives, enduring symbols, and modern trends that contribute to the rich mosaic of love expressions worldwide. Join us as we delve deeper into the intricate dance between the global and the local in the realm of Valentine's Day celebrations across borders.

Chapter 5: Love Across Time and Cultures
Historical Perspectives on Global Love Traditions

Love has been a constant in human history, transcending time and cultural boundaries. In this chapter, we embark on a journey through the annals of history, exploring how different societies across the globe have conceptualized and celebrated love. From ancient civilizations to medieval courts and beyond, historical perspectives on love traditions reveal the diverse ways in which affection, romance, and commitment have been expressed and understood throughout the ages.

Love in Ancient Civilizations: Foundations of Affection

The roots of love traditions can be traced back to ancient civilizations where diverse cultures laid the foundations for expressions of affection. In Mesopotamia, for example, the Epic of Gilgamesh provides insights into the complexities of love and friendship. Meanwhile, ancient Egypt revered the concept of marital love, as evidenced by the love poetry inscribed on tombs. These early societies embedded love in their cultural narratives, paving the way for the rich tapestry of love expressions that would unfold across time.

Classical Greece: Eros, Agape, and Platonic Ideals

Classical Greece introduced nuanced concepts of love that continue to influence cultural perceptions today. The Greeks distinguished between various forms of love, including Eros (romantic love), Agape (unconditional love or charity), and Platonic love (non-romantic affection). These distinctions laid the groundwork for philosophical discussions on the nature of love, exploring its emotional, spiritual, and intellectual dimensions.

Roman Influence: Marriage, Family, and Amor

With the rise of the Roman Empire, love took on different dimensions. The Romans valued the institution of marriage as a social and economic contract, while also celebrating the passionate aspects of love through the deity Amor. Love became entwined with familial and societal structures, and the concept of "civitas" emphasized the duty of citizens to contribute to the well-being of the state, including through family life.

Medieval Courtly Love: Romantic Idealism and Chivalry

The medieval period introduced the concept of courtly love, a romantic idealism that emerged within the aristocratic courts of Europe. Knights and troubadours extolled the virtues of chivalry and romantic devotion. This era saw the rise of literary works like "The Romance of the Rose," which explored the complexities of love, often in allegorical and symbolic terms. Courtly love laid the groundwork for the romantic traditions that would later influence Valentine's Day.

Islamic Golden Age: Love, Poetry, and Mysticism

During the Islamic Golden Age, love found expression through poetry and mysticism. Influential poets like Rumi wrote extensively on the theme of divine love, exploring the spiritual dimensions of affection. Love became a central theme in Sufi mysticism, with practitioners using metaphors of love and longing to describe their relationship with the divine. This era contributed to a rich literary tradition that elevated love to a sublime and transcendent experience.

Renaissance and Humanism: Rediscovering Antiquity

The Renaissance witnessed a revival of interest in classical ideals, including those related to love. Humanist thinkers drew inspiration from ancient Greek and Roman texts, reintroducing concepts like Platonic love and celebrating the beauty and complexity of human emotions. Art and literature from this period reflect a fascination with the intertwining of love, beauty, and the human experience.

18th and 19th Centuries: Romanticism and Sentimentality

The 18th and 19th centuries saw the rise of Romanticism, a cultural movement that emphasized emotion, individualism, and the sublime. Love took center stage in literature, music, and art, with a focus on intense emotions and the celebration of nature. The Victorian era, in particular, embraced sentimentality and elaborate expressions of affection, influencing the emergence of the modern Valentine's Day.

Cultural Variations: Love Traditions Around the World

As we move into more recent history, the 20th century and beyond, love traditions continued to evolve in diverse ways across the globe. In Japan, for example, the concept of "kokuhaku" involves the confession of romantic feelings, while India's rich cultural tapestry includes traditional arranged marriages alongside modern expressions of love. The global landscape of love traditions reflects the intricate interplay between cultural continuity and adaptation to changing times.

Impact of Wars and Movements: Love in Turbulent Times

The 20th century, marked by world wars and social movements, had a profound impact on love traditions. Wars separated couples, giving rise to poignant love letters and the symbolism of waiting for loved ones to return. Social movements, such as the sexual revolution and feminist movements, challenged traditional norms and reshaped societal attitudes toward love, autonomy, and partnership.

Technological Revolution: Love in the Digital Age

The technological revolution of the late 20th and early 21st centuries transformed the landscape of love. Communication technologies, from letters to emails, and now social media platforms, have altered the way people express affection across distances. Online dating and the globalization of popular culture have further interconnected societies, influencing the ways in which individuals navigate relationships and express love.

Cultural Resilience: Preserving and Adapting Love Traditions

Throughout history, love traditions have demonstrated remarkable resilience. Societies have preserved cultural expressions of affection while adapting to changing circumstances. This resilience is evident in the continued celebration of diverse love customs worldwide, including the coexistence of traditional practices with modern influences.

Conclusion: Love as a Universal Human Experience

Historical perspectives on global love traditions reveal a common thread—the universality of love as a human experience. Despite the diversity of cultural expressions, love has persisted as a fundamental aspect of the human condition. As we explore the intricacies of love across time and cultures, we gain a deeper understanding of the enduring and evolving nature of affectionate connections. In the chapters that follow, we will continue to unravel the complexities of love, examining enduring symbols, modern trends, and controversies surrounding its global celebration. Join us on this journey through history and across borders as we explore the rich tapestry of love traditions that define the human experience.

Timeless Themes in Cross-Cultural Love Stories

Love stories have transcended time and culture, weaving a tapestry of shared human experiences that resonate across borders. In this chapter, we delve into the timeless themes that permeate cross-cultural love narratives. From epic tales of passion to intimate portrayals of everyday romances, these stories reveal the enduring and universal aspects of love that connect us all.

Epic Love Stories: From Antiquity to Modernity

Epic love stories have been a recurring theme in the narratives of diverse cultures. Whether it's the tragic love of Romeo and Juliet in Shakespearean drama, the enduring loyalty of Laila and Majnun in Persian literature, or the timeless tale of Radha and Krishna in Hindu mythology, these stories capture the imagination and emotions of audiences across the globe. The universality of themes such as forbidden love, sacrifice, and destiny underscores the timeless nature of these narratives.

Folktales and Fairy Tales: Love Beyond Boundaries

Folktales and fairy tales are rich sources of cross-cultural love stories. Cinderella's transformative journey, the enduring love of Beauty and the Beast, or the perseverance of East Asian folklore's The Cowherd and the Weaver Girl—these tales transcend cultural differences to convey universal messages about the transformative power of love, the triumph of good over evil, and the belief in happily ever after.

Tragic Love: Sacrifice and Resilience

Tragedy has often been interwoven with love stories, illustrating the depth of human emotions and the sacrifices made in the name of love. Whether it's the Greek myth of Orpheus and Eurydice, the Shakespearean tragedy of Othello and Desdemona, or the 20th-century tale of Titanic's Jack and Rose, these stories explore the complexities of love, loss, and enduring resilience in the face of tragedy.

Cultural Icons of Love: Legends and Symbolism

Across cultures, certain individuals have become iconic symbols of love. From the legendary Persian poet Rumi, whose verses on love and mysticism resonate globally, to the Chinese folklore figure of the Butterfly Lovers, these cultural icons transcend their origins, becoming sources of inspiration for generations. The symbolism associated with these figures speaks to the enduring power of love to inspire and connect people across cultural boundaries.

Arranged Marriages and Enduring Partnerships

In many cultures, arranged marriages have been a longstanding tradition, emphasizing the importance of familial and community involvement in the union of individuals. Love in these contexts often unfolds over time, as couples navigate the complexities of shared lives. The enduring nature of partnerships formed through arranged marriages challenges Western notions of spontaneous, romantic love, illustrating that love can blossom and deepen in diverse ways.

Rebellious Love: Defying Social Norms

Some love stories are characterized by a defiance of societal norms and expectations. The iconic love affair between Cleopatra and Mark Antony challenged political conventions, while the clandestine romance of Heer and Ranjha in Punjabi folklore transcended social barriers. These narratives explore the themes of rebellion, passion, and the transformative power of love in the face of societal constraints.

Multicultural Love: Crossing Ethnic and Racial Boundaries

In an increasingly interconnected world, love stories that traverse ethnic and racial boundaries have gained prominence. The film "West Side Story," inspired by Shakespeare's Romeo and Juliet, portrays the challenges of love in a multicultural urban setting. Contemporary narratives, such as the novel "The Sun Is Also a Star" by Nicola Yoon, explore the complexities of love between individuals from different cultural backgrounds, highlighting the resilience of love in the face of diversity.

Love and War: Bonds Amidst Conflict

War has often served as a backdrop for love stories, illuminating the profound impact of conflict on human relationships. The enduring love between Odysseus and Penelope in Homer's "The Odyssey," the wartime romance of Allied soldiers and their sweethearts during World War II, or the contemporary exploration of love amidst conflict in novels like "The Kite Runner" by Khaled Hosseini—all these stories speak to the resilience of love in the most challenging circumstances.

Spiritual Love: Devotion Beyond the Physical

Many cultures incorporate spiritual dimensions into their love narratives, emphasizing the connection between love and a higher purpose. The Bhakti movement in India, which emphasizes love and devotion to a divine figure, exemplifies this spiritual approach to love. Similarly, Sufi poetry and the Christian concept of agape love explore the transcendent and selfless aspects of affection that go beyond the physical realm.

Everyday Romances: Ordinary Lives, Extraordinary Love

Not all love stories are grand or dramatic; some find beauty in the simplicity of everyday romances. These stories celebrate the ordinary moments shared between individuals— the quiet companionship of an elderly couple, the enduring love between childhood sweethearts, or the mutual support between partners in the routine of daily life. These narratives remind us that love's magic often lies in the mundane.

Cross-Cultural Adaptations: Global Influence on Local Narratives

As cultures interact and influence each other in the modern era, love stories have become increasingly globalized. Shakespeare's plays are performed in numerous languages, Bollywood films are watched worldwide, and international novels explore diverse love narratives. These cross-cultural adaptations reflect the interconnectedness of human experiences and the shared appreciation for the exploration of love in its myriad forms.

Conclusion: Love's Enduring Thread

Timeless themes in cross-cultural love stories reveal a common thread—a shared human experience that transcends geographical and temporal boundaries. Whether rooted in mythology, folklore, literature, or everyday life, these narratives illustrate that love, in its various forms, is a universal language. In the chapters that follow, we will continue to explore the intricacies of love, examining enduring symbols, modern trends, and controversies surrounding its global celebration. Join us on this journey through the realms of timeless love stories that have shaped the collective human understanding of affection across time and cultures.

Love as a Universal Human Experience

Love is a universal language that transcends cultural, temporal, and geographical boundaries. In this chapter, we delve into the profound idea that love is a core aspect of the human experience, exploring how it manifests in diverse ways across time and cultures. From the ancient expressions of affection to modern interpretations, the concept of love serves as a common thread weaving through the rich tapestry of human history.

Love as an Innate Human Emotion

At its core, love is recognized as an innate human emotion that forms a fundamental part of the human experience. From the earliest records of human history, expressions of affection and attachment have been documented, highlighting the instinctual nature of love. Whether in the form of familial bonds, friendships, or romantic partnerships, love emerges as a defining feature of what it means to be human.

Familial Love: The Foundation of Human Connection

Familial love stands as the bedrock of human relationships, forming the first bonds individuals experience. Across cultures, the love between parents and children, siblings, and extended family members is a universal constant. The care, protection, and nurturing associated with familial love provide the foundation for individuals to navigate the complexities of other forms of affection.

Friendship: Companionship Beyond Blood Ties

Friendship, often referred to as a chosen family, is another universal manifestation of love. Cultures around the world celebrate the bonds of camaraderie, mutual support, and shared experiences that characterize friendships. Whether through the ancient Greek concept of "philia" or the Confucian emphasis on virtuous friendships, societies recognize and value the importance of non-familial yet deeply meaningful connections.

Romantic Love: Cultural Expressions of Passion

Romantic love, with its intensity and passion, is a cultural theme that has manifested differently throughout history. From the courtly love of medieval Europe to the passionate expressions found in Latin American literature, each culture brings its unique nuances to the concept of romantic love. The universal experience of falling in love, navigating relationships, and expressing affection is a shared human journey.

Selfless Love: Sacrifice and Altruism

Love is often associated with selflessness and altruism, where individuals go beyond personal interests to prioritize the well-being of others. This aspect of love is evident in the sacrifices made by parents for their children, the dedication of caregivers, and the altruistic acts that transcend cultural and temporal boundaries. The theme of selfless love underscores the interconnectedness of humanity.

Love in Literature and Art: A Cross-Cultural Exploration

Throughout history, literature and art have served as powerful mediums for expressing and exploring the complexities of love. From the sonnets of Shakespeare to the verses of classical Persian poetry, cultural expressions of love have been immortalized in artistic creations. Paintings, sculptures, and music also capture the myriad emotions associated with love, offering a cross-cultural exploration of this universal theme.

Religious and Spiritual Love: Connecting with the Divine

Religious and spiritual traditions often emphasize the concept of divine love, linking the human experience of affection with a higher purpose. Whether it's the Christian notion of God's love, the Hindu understanding of divine devotion, or the Sufi mysticism that equates love with a spiritual journey, religious teachings highlight the transcendental and transformative nature of love.

Love's Role in Cultural Rituals and Traditions

Cultural rituals and traditions are imbued with expressions of love, marking significant milestones and life events. From wedding ceremonies that symbolize the union of two individuals in love to rituals honoring ancestors and celebrating community bonds, cultural practices reflect the importance of love in shaping collective identities and shared experiences.

Expressions of Love in Daily Life: Rituals and Gestures

Beyond grand ceremonies and epic tales, love permeates everyday life through rituals and gestures. Whether it's the act of sharing a meal, exchanging gifts, or offering a kind word, the small expressions of love in daily interactions contribute to the fabric of human connection. These gestures, often culturally influenced, underscore the universality of love in ordinary moments.

Emotional Intelligence: Understanding and Navigating Love

The ability to understand and navigate the complexities of love is an integral aspect of emotional intelligence—a trait universally valued across cultures. From recognizing and managing one's own emotions to empathizing with others, emotional intelligence plays a crucial role in fostering healthy relationships and creating harmonious communities.

Modern Challenges to Love: Navigating Change and Diversity

In the modern era, love faces new challenges shaped by technological advances, globalization, and evolving social norms. The digital age has redefined how individuals connect and form relationships, presenting both opportunities and challenges. Cultural diversity, while enriching the global tapestry of love, also requires individuals to navigate differences in values, expectations, and expressions of affection.

Love's Resilience: Enduring Amidst Change

Despite the evolving landscape of human interactions, love remains a resilient force that withstands the test of time and adapts to changing circumstances. The enduring nature of love is evident in its ability to transcend cultural shifts, technological advancements, and societal transformations. Love's resilience underscores its status as a timeless and universal element of the human experience.

Conclusion: Love's Universal Threads

Love, in its multifaceted expressions, serves as a universal thread that weaves through the diverse narratives of human history. From the ancient bonds of familial love to the modern complexities of romantic relationships, the concept of love transcends cultural, temporal, and geographical boundaries. In the chapters that follow, we will continue to unravel the intricacies of love, exploring enduring symbols, modern trends, and controversies surrounding its global celebration. Join us on this journey through the universality of love as a fundamental and timeless aspect of the human experience.

Influence of Ancient Cultures on Modern Love

The echoes of ancient cultures resonate in the contemporary expressions of love, shaping our understanding and practices in profound ways. In this chapter, we explore how the beliefs, rituals, and philosophical perspectives on love from ancient civilizations continue to influence modern relationships. From the enduring wisdom of classical philosophers to the symbolic rituals rooted in antiquity, the impact of ancient cultures on modern love is a testament to the timeless nature of human connections.

Classical Wisdom on Love: Insights from Greek Philosophy

The rich tapestry of Greek philosophy provides foundational insights into the nature of love that endure to this day. Philosophers like Plato explored the various dimensions of love through dialogues such as the "Symposium." The distinctions between Eros, Agape, and Platonic love introduced by these ancient thinkers continue to influence contemporary discussions on romantic and altruistic love. The enduring questions posed by philosophers about the essence of love, its forms, and its connection to higher ideals shape modern contemplations on the subject.

Roman Influence on Love and Marriage: Legacies of the Empire

The Roman Empire left an indelible mark on the institution of marriage and the expression of love. The concept of marriage as a social and legal contract, rooted in Roman traditions, has persisted through the ages. The celebration of weddings, the exchange of rings, and the legal frameworks surrounding marital unions owe a debt to Roman influences. The endurance of these practices highlights the lasting impact of ancient Roman culture on contemporary notions of love and commitment.

Ancient Eastern Philosophies: Love as Harmony and Balance

Eastern philosophies, such as those rooted in Hinduism, Buddhism, and Confucianism, offer distinctive perspectives on love as an integral part of the cosmic order. The emphasis on harmony, balance, and interconnectedness in these philosophies informs modern notions of love as a force that binds individuals and communities. Concepts like "dharma" and the interconnectedness of all beings continue to resonate in discussions about love's role in fostering societal cohesion and personal fulfillment.

Love in the Middle East: Arab Poetry and Islamic Traditions

The Middle East has a rich tradition of love poetry that has influenced the cultural expressions of affection. The works of poets like Rumi and the tales of Layla and Majnun convey profound messages about love as a transformative and spiritual experience. Islamic traditions, emphasizing love for God and compassion for fellow beings, contribute to the nuanced understanding of love in the modern Muslim world. These cultural and religious influences continue to shape the emotional landscape of the region.

Medieval Courtly Love: Chivalry and Romance Revisited

The medieval concept of courtly love, characterized by chivalry and romantic ideals, has left an enduring imprint on modern expressions of romance. The notions of romantic devotion, the pursuit of noble ideals, and the ritualized expressions of affection found in medieval literature influence contemporary narratives in art, literature, and popular culture. The themes of unrequited love, noble pursuits, and the transformative power of romantic ideals resonate in modern interpretations of love.

Influence of Renaissance Humanism: Love as a Cultural Ideal

The Renaissance era, marked by a revival of classical ideals, contributed to a reimagining of love as a cultural ideal. Humanist thinkers celebrated the beauty of human emotions and elevated the concept of romantic love in art and literature. The emphasis on individualism, emotional depth, and the celebration of love's transformative power during the Renaissance laid the groundwork for modern notions of intimate relationships and personal fulfillment.

Love in South Asian Traditions: Karma and Destiny

South Asian cultural traditions, deeply rooted in Hindu and Buddhist philosophies, contribute unique perspectives to the understanding of love. Concepts like "karma" and the idea of destined connections shape the narratives of love in South Asian cultures. The celebration of love as a cosmic force, intertwining the destinies of individuals, provides a distinct lens through which modern relationships in the region are often viewed.

Love in Indigenous Cultures: Nature, Community, and Connection

Indigenous cultures around the world bring their own perspectives on love, often deeply connected to nature, community, and ancestral wisdom. The symbiotic relationship between humans and the environment, celebrated in indigenous traditions, influences modern discourses on the interconnectedness of love, nature, and community. Rituals and ceremonies that honor these connections continue to inspire contemporary expressions of love grounded in a broader ecological and communal context.

Ancient Symbols of Love: Their Enduring Significance

Symbols rooted in ancient cultures continue to hold profound significance in modern expressions of love. From the enduring appeal of the heart shape, often associated with the ancient Greek concept of the "silphium" seed, to the symbolic meanings of flowers in different cultures, ancient symbols weave through contemporary expressions of affection. These symbols serve as bridges between the past and the present, carrying with them the weight of centuries of cultural significance.

Modern Adaptations and Challenges: Navigating Change

While ancient cultural influences persist, the modern era presents new challenges and adaptations in the realm of love. Technological advancements, changing social norms, and globalization introduce complexities that ancient cultures did not face. The interplay between traditional wisdom and contemporary challenges highlights the ongoing dialogue between the timeless aspects of love inherited from the past and the dynamic nature of relationships in the present.

Cultural Appropriation and Appreciation: Navigating Boundaries

As modern societies embrace elements of ancient cultures in expressions of love, the concepts of cultural appropriation and appreciation come to the fore. Navigating the boundaries between respectful incorporation and appropriation requires a nuanced understanding of the cultural context. This dynamic reflects the ongoing tension between preserving cultural authenticity and participating in the global conversation on love.

Conclusion: Love's Everlasting Echo

The influence of ancient cultures on modern love is an ever-present echo that resonates through the ages. Whether in the enduring wisdom of philosophers, the rituals of marriage, or the symbolic meanings embedded in cultural practices, ancient cultures have bequeathed a timeless legacy. As we continue to explore the complexities of love in the chapters that follow, we will unravel the interwoven threads of the past and present, discovering how the echoes of ancient cultures shape the rich tapestry of contemporary love. Join us on this journey through time and across cultures as we navigate the landscapes of love, informed by the enduring wisdom of our ancestors.

Chapter 6: Modern Global Love Trends
Technological Influences on International Romance

The advent of technology has transformed the landscape of love, reshaping the ways in which individuals connect, communicate, and cultivate relationships on a global scale. In this chapter, we delve into the intricate web of technological influences on international romance. From the rise of online dating platforms to the impact of social media on long-distance connections, the fusion of technology and love has given rise to novel possibilities and challenges in the pursuit of romantic connections across borders.

The Rise of Online Dating: Beyond Geographical Boundaries

Online dating has emerged as a powerful catalyst for connecting individuals across the globe. Dating platforms have transcended geographical constraints, allowing people from diverse cultural backgrounds to discover and connect with potential partners. The accessibility and efficiency of online dating services have democratized the search for love, enabling individuals to explore relationships beyond their immediate surroundings.

Virtual Connections: Navigating Borders Through Video Calls

The evolution of communication technologies has brought video calls to the forefront of long-distance relationships. Platforms like Skype, Zoom, and FaceTime have become essential tools for couples separated by geographical distances. Video calls not only bridge the gap between physical locations but also enhance the quality of communication, allowing couples to share experiences and moments in a more intimate and immediate way.

Social Media's Impact on Relationship Dynamics

The pervasive influence of social media extends into the realm of romance, shaping how individuals present and perceive their relationships. Platforms like Facebook, Instagram, and Twitter have become spaces where couples share their love stories, milestones, and everyday moments. Social media not only facilitates connection but also introduces a new dimension to relationship dynamics, influencing perceptions of intimacy, jealousy, and self-disclosure.

Globalization of Dating Practices: Cultural Exchange in Romantic Pursuits

As individuals from diverse cultural backgrounds engage in globalized dating practices, a cultural exchange occurs in the realm of romance. Cross-cultural relationships, facilitated by online platforms, provide opportunities for individuals to learn about and appreciate different customs, traditions, and perspectives on love. The intersection of diverse cultural influences in romantic connections contributes to the enrichment of global love narratives.

Challenges of Online Dating: Navigating Virtual Realities

While online dating opens up possibilities for international romance, it also poses unique challenges. The digital nature of interactions may lead to misunderstandings, misrepresentations, or a lack of authenticity. Navigating the transition from virtual connections to in-person relationships requires careful consideration of cultural nuances, communication styles, and the impact of technology on the dynamics of intimacy.

The Role of Dating Apps: Convenience and Choice

Dating apps have become integral to the modern romantic experience, offering users a convenient and diverse array of potential matches. The swipe culture introduced by apps like Tinder has revolutionized how people initiate connections, emphasizing visual appeal and shared interests. The accessibility of dating apps transcends borders, allowing individuals to explore romantic possibilities beyond their immediate social circles.

Navigating Cultural Differences: The Challenge of Global Love

As individuals engage in international romance facilitated by technology, they encounter the complexities of navigating cultural differences. Differences in communication styles, relationship expectations, and societal norms can pose challenges to cross-cultural relationships. Developing cultural competence and open communication become essential skills for those seeking love across borders.

Long-Distance Relationships in the Digital Age: Opportunities and Challenges

Long-distance relationships have been both facilitated and challenged by the digital age. While technology enables constant communication, the absence of physical proximity can present emotional and practical challenges. Virtual dates, online games, and shared digital experiences offer creative ways for couples to maintain a sense of closeness, but the endurance of long-distance relationships requires a commitment to communication and trust.

Technological Impact on Intimacy: Balancing Connection and Disconnection

The digital era has brought about a paradoxical impact on intimacy in romantic relationships. On one hand, technology facilitates constant connection through messaging, video calls, and social media. On the other hand, the omnipresence of technology can lead to a sense of disconnection when partners prioritize screens over face-to-face interactions. Balancing the benefits and drawbacks of technology in fostering intimacy becomes a key consideration in modern relationships.

Influence of Dating Shows and Media Representations

Dating shows and media representations of romance play a significant role in shaping cultural perceptions of love. Globalization has led to the international popularity of dating reality shows, influencing societal norms and expectations. These representations, often influenced by Western media, contribute to the globalization of dating practices and impact how individuals approach love in different cultural contexts.

The Dark Side of Online Connections: Scams and Deception

The anonymity afforded by online platforms has given rise to a dark side of international romance—online scams and deception. Catfishing, financial fraud, and other forms of online deceit pose risks to individuals seeking love online. Navigating the digital realm requires vigilance and awareness of potential pitfalls, highlighting the need for responsible and ethical engagement in online dating.

Virtual Celebrations and Shared Experiences: Redefining Togetherness

Technology has redefined how couples celebrate special occasions and share experiences despite physical distances. Virtual celebrations, whether through video calls, online games, or shared movie nights, allow couples to create moments of togetherness. The digital realm becomes a space for cultivating shared memories and maintaining a sense of connection during festive occasions and milestones.

The Future of International Romance: Technology and Beyond

As technology continues to advance, the future of international romance holds both exciting possibilities and challenges. Virtual reality, artificial intelligence, and augmented reality may further reshape how individuals connect romantically. However, the enduring importance of genuine communication, cultural understanding, and emotional connection will remain foundational elements in the evolving landscape of global love.

Conclusion: Navigating Love in the Digital Era

The intersection of technology and international romance unveils a dynamic landscape of possibilities and challenges. From the globalization of dating practices to the impact of social media on relationship dynamics, technology has become an integral part of the modern romantic experience. As we navigate the complexities of love in the digital era, the chapters that follow will explore additional facets of global love trends, shedding light on enduring symbols, controversies, and the evolving nature of connections across borders. Join us on this journey through the intersection of love and technology, where the digital realm becomes a canvas for the diverse expressions of romance in a globalized world.

Social Media's Role in Cross-Cultural Connections

In the digital age, social media has emerged as a powerful force shaping the landscape of love and relationships on a global scale. This chapter explores the multifaceted role of social media in facilitating cross-cultural connections, influencing how individuals navigate the complexities of international romance. From the impact on relationship dynamics to the way people present and perceive their love stories, social media has become an integral part of the modern love narrative.

The Global Stage of Social Media: Connecting Hearts Across Borders

Social media platforms serve as a virtual global stage where individuals from different corners of the world can connect, interact, and build relationships. Platforms like Facebook, Instagram, Twitter, and others transcend geographical boundaries, providing a space for cross-cultural connections to flourish. As people share their lives, interests, and values online, social media becomes a bridge that brings together diverse individuals seeking love and companionship.

Cross-Cultural Exposure: Expanding Horizons Through Digital Connections

One of the profound impacts of social media on cross-cultural connections is the exposure to diverse perspectives, lifestyles, and cultural nuances. Through the content shared on platforms, individuals gain insights into the daily lives, traditions, and beliefs of people from other parts of the world. This exposure fosters cultural curiosity and understanding, laying the foundation for cross-cultural relationships to flourish.

Digital Storytelling: Narratives of Love Across Cultures

Social media platforms serve as digital canvases for individuals to craft and share their love stories. From the first virtual encounter to milestones in the relationship, couples use social media to narrate their journeys. This digital storytelling not only documents the personal narrative but also provides a window into the ways in which love is expressed, experienced, and celebrated across diverse cultural backgrounds.

Language of Love: Communicating Across Linguistic Barriers

The diverse linguistic landscape of social media reflects the richness of cross-cultural connections. Multilingual interactions become a common feature in globalized digital spaces, allowing individuals to communicate and express affection across linguistic barriers. Emojis, stickers, and multimedia content contribute to a universal language of love that transcends spoken and written words, fostering a sense of connection in a global community.

Online Communities: Creating Spaces for Cross-Cultural Love

Social media platforms host a myriad of online communities where individuals with shared interests, including cross-cultural relationships, come together. These communities provide a supportive space for people to share experiences, seek advice, and connect with others navigating similar cross-cultural dynamics. The sense of community fosters a feeling of belonging and understanding among individuals engaged in or considering cross-cultural relationships.

Navigating Cultural Differences in the Digital Sphere

While social media facilitates cross-cultural connections, it also introduces challenges related to navigating cultural differences. Individuals engaging in cross-cultural relationships through digital platforms must navigate varying cultural norms, communication styles, and relationship expectations. The digital realm becomes a dynamic space where cultural awareness, open communication, and respect for diversity are essential in fostering healthy cross-cultural connections.

Social Media and Relationship Dynamics: The Impact on Intimacy

The integration of social media into romantic relationships influences the dynamics of intimacy. Platforms offer new avenues for expressing affection, staying connected, and sharing intimate moments. However, the constant presence of social media also poses challenges, as couples navigate issues of privacy, jealousy, and the potential for miscommunication. Balancing the benefits and drawbacks becomes crucial in maintaining a healthy and intimate connection.

Love in the Spotlight: Influencers and Relationship Goals

The rise of social media influencers has brought love and relationships into the public eye. Couples who share their romantic journeys online become influencers, shaping societal perceptions of idealized relationships. The concept of "relationship goals" permeates social media, influencing how individuals perceive and aspire to construct their own love stories. The impact of influencer couples on shaping cultural expectations of love becomes a noteworthy aspect of modern cross-cultural connections.

Social Media PDA: Public Displays of Affection Across Borders

Public displays of affection (PDA) take on new dimensions in the digital era, where couples share their love openly on social media. The digital realm becomes a space for expressing affection, celebrating anniversaries, and showcasing the highs of the relationship. This public sharing, however, requires a delicate balance to respect cultural sensitivities and preferences regarding the private nature of romantic relationships.

Challenges of Digital Intimacy: Screen-Mediated Love

The digital nature of cross-cultural connections introduces challenges related to screen-mediated intimacy. While technology allows couples to bridge geographical gaps, it also presents the risk of a disconnect between the virtual and physical realms. Navigating the balance between digital interactions and in-person intimacy becomes a consideration for individuals engaged in cross-cultural relationships facilitated by social media.

Social Media and Cultural Appropriation: Navigating Boundaries

As individuals share aspects of their cross-cultural relationships on social media, questions of cultural appropriation and appreciation come to the forefront. Navigating the boundaries between sharing personal experiences and respecting cultural authenticity becomes a nuanced aspect of digital storytelling. Responsible and ethical engagement in the digital space requires sensitivity to cultural nuances and a commitment to promoting understanding.

Social Media and Long-Distance Love: Bridging the Emotional Gap

For couples in long-distance cross-cultural relationships, social media becomes a lifeline for maintaining emotional closeness. Regular communication through messaging, video calls, and virtual shared experiences helps bridge the emotional gap created by physical distance. The digital tools provided by social media offer creative solutions for fostering connection and intimacy across borders.

The Future of Cross-Cultural Love on Social Media

As social media continues to evolve, the future of cross-cultural love on digital platforms holds both promises and challenges. Advances in augmented reality, virtual reality, and interactive features may further enhance the ways in which individuals connect romantically across borders. However, the core principles of understanding, respect, and effective communication will remain integral to the success of cross-cultural relationships facilitated by social media.

Conclusion: Love in the Digital Crossroads

Social media's role in cross-cultural connections marks a transformative intersection of technology and love. From fostering global communities to influencing relationship dynamics and cultural perceptions of love, social media shapes the narrative of cross-cultural romance. As we navigate the complexities of love in the digital age, the chapters that follow will explore additional facets of modern global love trends, shedding light on enduring symbols, controversies, and the evolving nature of connections across borders. Join us on this journey through the digital crossroads of love, where social media becomes a dynamic force in the pursuit of cross-cultural connections.

Globalization of Dating Practices

In the interconnected world of the 21st century, the pursuit of love and companionship has transcended geographical boundaries, ushering in a new era of globalized dating practices. This chapter explores the various facets of how dating has evolved into a global phenomenon, shaped by cultural exchange, technological advancements, and shifting societal norms. From the rise of international online platforms to the fusion of traditional and modern dating customs, the globalization of dating practices reflects the dynamic nature of contemporary relationships.

Introduction: The Shifting Landscape of Dating in a Globalized World

In the not-so-distant past, dating was often confined to local communities and social circles. However, the advent of globalization has redefined the landscape of romantic connections, breaking down barriers and creating a global stage for individuals to seek love. This section introduces the transformative journey of dating practices from localized to globalized, setting the stage for an exploration of the key factors influencing this shift.

The Rise of International Online Dating Platforms

Online dating platforms have emerged as the vanguards of the globalized dating revolution. These platforms transcend national borders, providing individuals with the opportunity to connect with potential partners from diverse cultural backgrounds. The accessibility and efficiency of international dating apps and websites have transformed the way people approach relationships, ushering in an era where geographical constraints are no longer significant obstacles to finding love.

Cross-Cultural Relationships: Embracing Diversity in Love

One of the hallmark features of the globalization of dating practices is the rise of cross-cultural relationships. Individuals are increasingly open to exploring romantic connections with partners from different countries and cultural backgrounds. This shift reflects a growing appreciation for diversity and a recognition that love knows no borders. Cross-cultural relationships bring together individuals with unique perspectives, traditions, and worldviews, contributing to a richer tapestry of global love stories.

Cultural Exchange in Romantic Pursuits: Learning and Appreciating Differences

Globalized dating practices facilitate cultural exchange in romantic pursuits. Individuals engaged in cross-cultural relationships often find themselves exposed to new traditions, languages, and ways of expressing affection. This section explores how the exploration of cultural differences becomes an integral part of modern dating, fostering understanding, appreciation, and personal growth among individuals seeking love on a global scale.

Navigating Language Barriers: The Universal Language of Love

As individuals engage in globalized dating, they often encounter language barriers. The universal language of love, however, transcends linguistic differences. This section delves into how couples navigate communication challenges, using various tools and strategies to express affection, build connections, and forge meaningful relationships despite linguistic diversity. The role of technology and translation tools in breaking down language barriers becomes a crucial aspect of globalized dating.

Blending Tradition and Modernity: Fusion of Dating Customs

The globalization of dating practices has led to the fusion of traditional and modern customs. As individuals from different cultural backgrounds come together, they bring with them a blend of inherited traditions and contemporary dating norms. This section explores how the amalgamation of diverse dating customs contributes to the evolution of globalized romance, creating unique and hybrid approaches to courtship and relationships.

Long-Distance Relationships in a Globalized World

The globalized nature of modern dating often results in long-distance relationships. Geographical separation, once considered a significant challenge, has become a common aspect of many romantic connections. This section delves into the dynamics of long-distance relationships in a globalized world, exploring the impact of technology, communication strategies, and the emotional resilience required to sustain love across borders.

Globalization and Changing Gender Dynamics in Dating

The globalization of dating practices is accompanied by shifts in gender dynamics. Traditional gender roles are being redefined as individuals from diverse cultural backgrounds interact on global platforms. This section examines how changing perceptions of gender roles influence dating behaviors, expectations, and power dynamics in relationships. The evolving landscape of gender equality becomes a crucial factor in understanding the dynamics of modern globalized dating.

Globalized Dating and Cultural Sensitivity: Navigating Challenges

While globalized dating brings diverse individuals together, it also presents challenges related to cultural sensitivity. This section explores how individuals navigate cultural nuances, avoid stereotypes, and foster respectful interactions in cross-cultural relationships. Sensitivity to cultural differences becomes an essential skill for those engaged in globalized dating, fostering harmonious and meaningful connections.

The Influence of Western Media on Global Love Trends

The dominance of Western media, particularly Hollywood, has played a significant role in shaping global perceptions of love and romance. This section examines how Western cultural influences impact dating practices around the world. From cinematic portrayals of love to the global popularity of Western relationship ideals, the influence of Western media becomes a noteworthy factor in the globalization of dating norms.

Ethical Considerations in Globalized Dating: Navigating Intersections

As individuals engage in globalized dating practices, ethical considerations come to the forefront. This section explores issues of cultural appropriation, respectful engagement, and responsible representation in the digital realm. Navigating the ethical dimensions of cross-cultural relationships becomes an integral aspect of ensuring that globalized dating practices promote understanding, inclusivity, and authenticity.

Conclusion: Love Without Borders - The Future of Globalized Dating

The globalization of dating practices has transformed the landscape of love, ushering in an era where individuals can seek companionship beyond geographical constraints. This concluding section reflects on the key themes explored in the chapter, highlighting the evolving nature of globalized dating. As we look toward the future, the chapter concludes with insights into the continued impact of globalization on dating practices and the enduring pursuit of love without borders. Join us on this journey through the changing contours of modern romance, where globalized dating practices redefine how individuals connect, create, and experience love in an interconnected world.

Influence of Western Media on Global Love Trends

The globalization of love is intricately intertwined with the influence of Western media, particularly Hollywood, which has played a pivotal role in shaping romantic narratives and relationship ideals worldwide. This section delves into the profound impact of Western media on global love trends, exploring how cinematic portrayals, cultural exports, and relationship ideals propagated through media have shaped the expectations and behaviors of individuals in their pursuit of love across cultures.

Cinematic Portrayals of Love: Hollywood's Global Impact

Hollywood, as the epicenter of the global film industry, has significantly influenced perceptions of love and romance on a worldwide scale. Romantic movies produced in Hollywood often serve as cultural ambassadors, spreading ideals of love, passion, and companionship. This section examines the enduring influence of Hollywood's cinematic portrayals of love, exploring how these narratives shape societal expectations and contribute to the globalized understanding of romantic relationships.

Global Popularity of Western Rom-Coms: Cultural Homogenization or Diversity?

The romantic comedy genre, a staple of Western cinema, has achieved global popularity, transcending cultural and linguistic barriers. This section analyzes the appeal of Western romantic comedies in diverse cultural contexts. It explores whether the widespread popularity of these films contributes to cultural homogenization, erasing unique cultural nuances, or if it allows for a celebration of diversity, with audiences adapting and integrating Western romantic tropes into their own cultural love narratives.

Exporting Relationship Ideals: Westernization of Love Norms

The export of Western relationship ideals through media goes beyond cinematic portrayals to influence societal norms and expectations. Westernized notions of love, romance, and relationships often permeate global cultures through television shows, music, and digital content. This section examines how the Westernization of love norms shapes the way individuals perceive and approach relationships, sometimes leading to a blending of traditional values with modern ideals.

The Role of Celebrity Culture: Icons of Western Romance

Celebrity couples from Western cultures often become global icons of love, shaping societal perceptions and expectations. This section explores the phenomenon of celebrity culture and its impact on global love trends. It examines how the relationships of Western celebrities, showcased in media and on social platforms, influence the way individuals perceive and model their own romantic relationships, contributing to the globalization of certain relationship norms.

Impact of Western Dating Shows: A Global Phenomenon

The proliferation of Western dating reality shows has turned the quest for love into a global phenomenon. Programs like "The Bachelor" and "Love Island" have been adapted and localized in various countries, influencing dating behaviors and relationship dynamics. This section analyzes the impact of Western dating shows on global love trends, exploring how the format, values, and expectations portrayed in these shows shape the dating landscape worldwide.

The Globalization of Online Dating Apps: A Western Invention Goes Global

Online dating, a phenomenon that originated in the West, has become a globalized practice reshaping how individuals seek and find love. This section explores the journey of online dating apps, such as Tinder and OkCupid, from Western origins to worldwide ubiquity. It examines how these platforms export Westernized approaches to dating and relationships, impacting global perceptions of love and courtship.

Social Media Influencers: Shaping Relationship Goals Worldwide

Social media influencers, often rooted in Western cultures, have become powerful agents in shaping relationship goals on a global scale. This section investigates how influencers, through platforms like Instagram and YouTube, curate and share their love stories, influencing followers worldwide. It explores the impact of these influencers on shaping cultural expectations of love and relationships, creating a digital space for the globalization of relationship ideals.

Challenges of Western Cultural Dominance: Cultural Appropriation and Resistance

The dominance of Western media in shaping global love trends raises questions of cultural appropriation and resistance. This section examines how individuals and cultures navigate the challenges of adopting Westernized relationship ideals while preserving their own cultural authenticity. It explores instances of resistance, reinterpretation, and the negotiation of cultural influences in the pursuit of love in a globalized world.

Representation Matters: Diverse Narratives in Global Media

While Western media has played a significant role in shaping global love trends, the importance of diverse representation cannot be overlooked. This section emphasizes the need for diverse narratives in global media, acknowledging the richness of love stories from different cultures. It explores how increased representation fosters a more inclusive and nuanced understanding of love, challenging the dominance of Western-centric ideals.

Navigating Cultural Sensitivity: A Call for Informed Consumption

Consumers of Western media must navigate cultural sensitivity to ensure respectful engagement with diverse narratives. This section discusses the responsibility of media consumers to approach Westernized portrayals of love with cultural awareness and a critical lens. It explores the potential for informed consumption to contribute to a more nuanced and inclusive global dialogue on love and relationships.

Conclusion: Navigating the Global Tapestry of Love

The influence of Western media on global love trends is a dynamic and complex phenomenon, shaping the collective imagination of romance on a worldwide scale. As we conclude this exploration, it becomes clear that while Western media has undeniably left an indelible mark, the global tapestry of love is woven with diverse threads. Moving forward, understanding, appreciating, and critiquing the impact of Western media on love trends is essential for fostering a global dialogue that celebrates the rich diversity of romantic narratives across cultures. Join us in the chapters that follow as we continue to unravel the intricacies of modern global love trends, exploring enduring symbols, controversies, and the evolving nature of connections across borders.

Chapter 7: Global Perspectives on Long-Distance Love
Navigating Love Across Borders and Oceans

In the intricate tapestry of global romance, long-distance love stands as a testament to the resilience of human connections that transcend geographical boundaries. This section delves into the nuances of navigating love across borders and oceans, exploring the challenges, triumphs, and unique dynamics that define relationships where physical proximity is a luxury.

Introduction: The Poetic Complexity of Long-Distance Love

Long-distance love is a poetic dance between hearts separated by miles but united by a shared commitment. In this introduction, we unravel the complexities that define the landscape of love that transcends borders and oceans. It sets the stage for an exploration of the unique challenges faced by couples separated by distance and the extraordinary ways in which they bridge the emotional gap.

The Geography of the Heart: Defying Physical Boundaries

In long-distance relationships, the geography of the heart defies the constraints of physical space. This section explores how individuals in love overcome the challenges of being separated by vast distances. It delves into the emotional landscape of long-distance love, where the heart's compass guides the journey of connection, intimacy, and commitment despite the oceans, mountains, and borders that lie in between.

Cultural Crossroads: Love in a Globalized World

Long-distance love often occurs at the crossroads of diverse cultures. Partners from different corners of the world bring their unique backgrounds, traditions, and perspectives into the relationship. This section explores how cultural diversity enriches the tapestry of long-distance love, fostering an environment where the exchange of traditions becomes an integral part of the romantic narrative.

Technological Ties: The Role of Communication in Distance

Technology emerges as the lifeline that sustains long-distance relationships. From video calls to instant messaging, this section delves into the crucial role of technology in bridging the communication gap between partners separated by borders and oceans. It explores how couples leverage digital tools to share moments, maintain intimacy, and create a sense of togetherness despite the physical distance.

Challenges of Temporal and Spatial Separation

Temporal and spatial separation in long-distance relationships introduces unique challenges. This section explores how partners navigate differences in time zones, synchronize schedules, and cope with the longing for physical presence. It delves into the emotional impact of temporal and spatial challenges, shedding light on the resilience required to sustain love across miles and hours.

Cross-Cultural Challenges: Navigating Differences

The cross-cultural dynamics of long-distance relationships bring both richness and challenges. Partners must navigate differences in communication styles, relationship expectations, and cultural norms. This section explores how couples manage the complexities of cross-cultural relationships, emphasizing the importance of cultural sensitivity, open communication, and mutual respect in fostering a strong and resilient connection.

Traveling Hearts: The Significance of Visits and Reunions

Visits and reunions become cherished milestones in the journey of long-distance love. This section examines the significance of physical meetings, exploring how partners navigate the anticipation, joy, and sometimes the bittersweet moments of saying goodbye. It highlights the transformative impact of in-person encounters on the emotional fabric of long-distance relationships.

Virtual Celebrations and Shared Moments

Celebrating special occasions and creating shared moments are integral to the vibrancy of long-distance love. This section explores how couples use virtual platforms to celebrate birthdays, anniversaries, and other milestones. It delves into the creativity and ingenuity required to make virtual celebrations memorable, emphasizing the power of shared experiences in fostering emotional closeness.

The Emotional Rollercoaster: Coping with Ups and Downs

Long-distance love is often characterized by emotional highs and lows. This section delves into the emotional rollercoaster that partners may experience – from the elation of a heartfelt message to the challenges of missing daily companionship. It explores coping mechanisms, emotional resilience, and the ways in which partners support each other through the peaks and valleys of long-distance relationships.

Building Trust Across Distances

Trust forms the bedrock of any strong relationship, and in the context of long-distance love, it takes on heightened significance. This section explores the dynamics of trust-building across distances, examining the challenges and strategies employed by couples to maintain a strong foundation of trust. It emphasizes the role of transparent communication, consistency, and mutual understanding in nurturing trust in long-distance relationships.

The Impact of Global Events: External Challenges to Love

External factors, such as global events, can have a profound impact on long-distance relationships. This section explores how unforeseen circumstances, such as pandemics, natural disasters, or geopolitical events, can disrupt plans, create additional stress, and test the resilience of long-distance love. It delves into the strategies partners employ to navigate external challenges and emerge stronger from shared trials.

Crossing Borders: Navigating Immigration and Legal Challenges

In some long-distance relationships, crossing borders involves navigating immigration and legal challenges. This section explores the complexities faced by couples dealing with visa restrictions, cultural differences in immigration processes, and the emotional toll of being separated by bureaucratic hurdles. It sheds light on the resilience and commitment required to overcome legal barriers in the pursuit of love.

Support Systems: The Role of Friends and Family

Friends and family play a crucial role in providing support to individuals in long-distance relationships. This section explores how external support systems contribute to the success of long-distance love. It examines the importance of understanding from loved ones, the impact of cultural differences on familial expectations, and the ways in which friends and family become pillars of strength for couples navigating distance.

Long-Term Planning: From Distance to Coexistence

Long-distance relationships often involve dreams of eventual coexistence. This section explores how partners in long-distance love engage in long-term planning, discussing aspirations, goals, and timelines for closing the distance. It delves into the challenges of making life-altering decisions, such as relocation, and the excitement that comes with envisioning a shared future beyond the constraints of geographical separation.

Conclusion: Love Knows No Borders

As we conclude this exploration of long-distance love across borders and oceans, it becomes evident that love, when nurtured with dedication and resilience, transcends the challenges posed by physical distances. The chapters that follow will continue to unravel the intricacies of global love trends, exploring enduring symbols, controversies, and the evolving nature of connections across borders. Join us in this journey through the diverse landscapes of modern romance, where love knows no borders and hearts remain connected despite the vastness of oceans and the boundaries that seek to separate them.

Cross-Cultural Challenges in Long-Distance Relationships

Long-distance relationships, inherently complex in their nature, take on an additional layer of intricacy when partners hail from different cultural backgrounds. Navigating the intricacies of cross-cultural challenges becomes an integral part of the journey, shaping the dynamics, communication, and overall experience of love that transcends borders. In this section, we delve into the unique challenges faced by couples in long-distance relationships where cultural diversity adds both richness and complexity to their shared narrative.

Introduction: The Interplay of Love and Culture in Distance

The intersection of love and culture in long-distance relationships introduces a unique set of dynamics. This introduction sets the stage for an exploration of the challenges that arise when partners from diverse cultural backgrounds navigate the complexities of being physically separated. It emphasizes the role of cultural sensitivity, open communication, and mutual understanding as essential elements in overcoming cross-cultural challenges in the context of long-distance love.

The Dance of Communication Styles: Bridging Verbal and Non-Verbal Gaps

Communication lies at the heart of any relationship, and in cross-cultural long-distance relationships, partners may grapple with differences in communication styles. This section explores how individuals from varying cultural backgrounds navigate verbal and non-verbal communication gaps. It delves into the nuances of expression, tone, and cultural cues that can impact the effectiveness of communication in long-distance love.

Cultural Norms and Relationship Expectations: Bridging the Divide

Cultural norms and expectations regarding relationships can differ significantly from one culture to another. This section examines how partners in cross-cultural long-distance relationships negotiate and navigate these differences. It explores the impact of cultural expectations on relationship milestones, expressions of affection, and the overall trajectory of the partnership, shedding light on the complexities inherent in aligning diverse cultural norms.

Religious and Traditions: Finding Common Ground or Navigating Differences

Diverse religious beliefs and cultural traditions can become focal points of both unity and challenge in cross-cultural long-distance relationships. This section explores how partners navigate the terrain of religious and traditional differences, whether by finding common ground, respecting each other's practices, or navigating potential tensions. It delves into the ways in which couples integrate diverse religious and cultural aspects into their relationship narratives.

Time Zones as Temporal Divides: Juggling Schedules Across Cultures

The temporal challenge of being in different time zones amplifies the complexities of cross-cultural long-distance relationships. This section examines how partners juggle schedules, coordinate virtual meetings, and bridge the temporal gap to maintain a sense of connection. It explores the impact of time zone differences on daily communication, the coordination of visits, and the emotional toll of being out of sync with each other's daily lives.

Navigating Language Barriers: Love in Multilingual Spaces

Language, a vehicle for communication and expression of emotions, can present both challenges and opportunities in cross-cultural long-distance relationships. This section explores how language barriers are navigated, whether partners speak different native languages or English serves as a common medium. It delves into the richness of multilingual love, exploring the ways in which language becomes an integral part of the cross-cultural relationship narrative.

Family Expectations: Balancing Individual and Cultural Dynamics

Family expectations, deeply rooted in cultural norms, can play a significant role in cross-cultural long-distance relationships. This section examines how partners balance individual desires with familial expectations. It explores the challenges of gaining acceptance from families with diverse cultural backgrounds, negotiating cultural differences, and fostering understanding among relatives who may hold varying perspectives on the relationship.

Celebrating Cultural Festivities: The Intersection of Traditions

Cross-cultural long-distance relationships often involve the celebration of diverse cultural festivities. This section explores how partners incorporate each other's cultural traditions into their relationship, whether through virtual celebrations or in-person gatherings during visits. It delves into the ways in which cultural festivities become a bridge that connects partners, fostering a deeper appreciation for each other's heritage.

Respecting Cultural Sensitivities: A Foundation for Understanding

Respecting and navigating cultural sensitivities form the bedrock of successful cross-cultural long-distance relationships. This section emphasizes the importance of cultural awareness, open-mindedness, and the willingness to learn and adapt. It explores how partners foster an environment of understanding, where cultural differences are not seen as obstacles but rather as opportunities for growth and shared experiences.

Conflict Resolution Across Cultures: Navigating Disagreements with Sensitivity

Disagreements and conflicts are natural aspects of any relationship, but in cross-cultural long-distance relationships, they may be compounded by diverse cultural perspectives on conflict resolution. This section explores how partners navigate disagreements with cultural sensitivity, considering diverse approaches to communication, negotiation, and resolution. It highlights the role of empathy and compromise in maintaining harmony across cultural divides.

Intersecting Identities: The Dynamics of Dual or Multiple Cultures

In cross-cultural long-distance relationships, individuals may find themselves navigating the dynamics of dual or multiple cultural identities. This section examines the complexities of partners who identify with more than one culture, exploring how these intersecting identities impact their perspectives, values, and the way they navigate the challenges of distance. It delves into the richness and challenges inherent in relationships where cultural identity is multifaceted.

Cultural Learning and Growth: A Shared Journey

Cross-cultural long-distance relationships offer partners the opportunity for continuous cultural learning and growth. This section explores how individuals enrich each other's lives by sharing and celebrating their respective cultures. It examines the ways in which partners become catalysts for cultural exploration, fostering a shared journey of learning, adaptation, and mutual appreciation for the diverse backgrounds that shape their identities.

Conclusion: Love Beyond Borders and Cultures

As we conclude our exploration of cross-cultural challenges in long-distance relationships, it is evident that love, when entwined with cultural diversity, becomes a dynamic and enriching journey. The chapters that follow will continue to unravel the intricacies of global love trends, exploring enduring symbols, controversies, and the evolving nature of connections across borders. Join us on this journey through the diverse landscapes of modern romance, where love knows no cultural boundaries, and hearts remain connected despite the complexities of cross-cultural challenges.

Shared Experiences in International Long-Distance Love

Long-distance relationships, particularly those spanning international borders, create a unique tapestry of shared experiences. Partners separated by miles and cultural differences navigate a journey marked by virtual connections, longing, and the anticipation of eventual reunions. In this section, we delve into the common threads that weave through the fabric of international long-distance love, exploring the shared experiences that define and strengthen these relationships.

Introduction: The Universality of Long-Distance Love

The introduction sets the stage for an exploration of shared experiences in international long-distance love, highlighting the universal aspects that bridge the gap between partners separated by geography and cultural diversity. It emphasizes the common threads that weave through the diverse narratives of couples navigating the challenges and joys of maintaining love across borders.

Virtual Togetherness: Navigating Intimacy Across Screens

Virtual communication becomes the lifeline of international long-distance love, providing a platform for partners to bridge the physical gap. This section explores how couples create a sense of togetherness through video calls, messages, and virtual shared activities. It delves into the ways in which technology fosters intimacy, allowing partners to connect emotionally despite the geographical distance.

The Language of Long-Distance Love: Expressing Affection Across Cultures

Expressions of love take on a special significance in international long-distance relationships, where partners may hail from different cultural backgrounds. This section examines how couples navigate the nuances of expressing affection, love languages, and the ways in which cultural differences may influence the articulation of emotions. It explores the creativity and adaptability required to communicate love across cultural and linguistic divides.

Counting Moments, Not Miles: Celebrating Milestones from Afar

International long-distance love often involves celebrating milestones and special moments from afar. This section explores how couples find creative ways to mark anniversaries, birthdays, and other significant occasions despite being separated by borders. It delves into the challenges of creating meaningful and memorable experiences, emphasizing the resilience and commitment required to maintain a sense of celebration.

Navigating Different Time Zones: The Temporal Dance of Connection

Time zone differences pose a unique challenge in international long-distance relationships. This section explores how partners navigate the temporal complexities, coordinating schedules, and finding moments of connection despite being in different parts of the world. It examines the impact of time zone variations on daily communication, the coordination of visits, and the emotional adjustments required to bridge temporal divides.

Traveling Virtually: Exploring New Cultures Together

International long-distance love often involves exploring each other's cultures, even from a distance. This section examines how partners virtually travel together, sharing insights into their respective worlds. It delves into the ways in which couples embrace cultural exchange, whether through virtual tours, language lessons, or cooking together, fostering a sense of connection through the exploration of diverse cultures.

The Emotional Rollercoaster: Highs and Lows in International Love

The emotional rollercoaster of highs and lows is a shared experience in international long-distance love. This section delves into the elation of joyful moments and the challenges of navigating the lows – the longing, loneliness, and occasional misunderstandings. It explores the emotional resilience required to sustain love across borders and cultures, highlighting the shared journey of emotional highs and lows that define these relationships.

Support Systems: Building a Network Across Continents

In international long-distance relationships, support systems play a crucial role in providing emotional sustenance. This section explores how partners build a network of friends and family across continents, seeking understanding and empathy from those who may be geographically distant but emotionally close. It examines the ways in which external support systems contribute to the strength and endurance of international long-distance love.

Cultural Fusion: Creating a Shared Identity

Cultural fusion becomes a defining aspect of international long-distance love, where partners blend their diverse backgrounds to create a shared identity. This section examines how couples navigate the complexities of merging cultural traditions, values, and practices. It explores the ways in which cultural fusion enriches the relationship narrative, fostering a unique and evolving shared identity.

The Anticipation of Reunions: Navigating the Journey Back to Each Other

The anticipation of reunions becomes a driving force in international long-distance love. This section explores how partners navigate the emotional journey leading up to the physical reunion, managing expectations, and savoring the excitement of being together again. It delves into the challenges and joys of transitioning from virtual to physical togetherness, emphasizing the transformative power of reunions in these relationships.

Challenges of International Travel: Navigating Practical Hurdles

International long-distance relationships often involve navigating the practical challenges of international travel. This section examines the hurdles partners face, including visa requirements, travel restrictions, and the financial implications of frequent international visits. It delves into the strategic planning and resilience required to overcome these challenges, underscoring the commitment to maintaining a connection despite logistical barriers.

Creating Shared Rituals: Anchors in the Sea of Distance

Shared rituals become anchors in the sea of distance, providing a sense of continuity and stability in international long-distance relationships. This section explores how partners establish routines, whether through shared activities, virtual dates, or daily check-ins, creating a foundation that withstands the challenges of geographical separation. It emphasizes the role of shared rituals in fostering a sense of normalcy and connection.

Building Dreams Across Borders: Planning a Shared Future

International long-distance relationships often involve dreaming and planning for a shared future. This section examines how partners navigate discussions about relocation, cultural adaptation, and building a life together. It delves into the challenges and excitement of envisioning a future beyond borders, emphasizing the shared commitment to building a life that integrates both partners' backgrounds and aspirations.

Conclusion: The Tapestry of International Long-Distance Love

As we conclude this exploration of shared experiences in international long-distance love, it is evident that the fabric of these relationships is woven with threads of creativity, resilience, and commitment. The chapters that follow will continue to unravel the intricacies of global love trends, exploring enduring symbols, controversies, and the evolving nature of connections across borders. Join us on this journey through the diverse landscapes of modern romance, where love knows no international boundaries, and hearts remain connected despite the vast distances that seek to separate them.

Virtual Celebrations and Connecting Beyond Boundaries

Long-distance relationships often necessitate innovative approaches to celebrating special occasions and fostering a sense of connection. In this section, we explore the role of virtual celebrations in international long-distance love, examining how couples bridge geographical gaps to create meaningful and memorable moments together. From birthdays to anniversaries, this exploration sheds light on the creativity and dedication that define the virtual celebrations shared by partners separated by borders.

Introduction: Celebrating Love in the Virtual Realm

The introduction sets the stage for an exploration of virtual celebrations as a dynamic element in international long-distance love. It emphasizes the importance of celebrating milestones, creating shared memories, and the unique challenges and opportunities presented by virtual platforms in maintaining a sense of togetherness despite physical separation.

The Virtual Birthday Bash: Celebrating Milestones from Afar

Birthdays are significant milestones in any relationship, and in international long-distance love, celebrating them becomes a creative endeavor. This section delves into how partners orchestrate virtual birthday celebrations, exploring the planning, surprises, and the use of technology to make the distance feel less significant on these special days. It highlights the emotional impact of virtually sharing the joy of birthdays across borders.

Anniversary Celebrations in the Virtual Space: Reflecting on Milestones

Anniversaries hold a special place in the hearts of couples, and in international long-distance relationships, marking these milestones becomes an art of reflection and connection. This section explores how partners commemorate anniversaries through virtual means, from heartfelt messages to creative surprises that transcend the limitations of physical distance. It emphasizes the role of virtual celebrations in strengthening the bond between partners separated by borders.

Virtual Date Nights: Recreating the Romance From Afar

Date nights are an integral part of romantic relationships, and in international long-distance love, they take on a virtual twist. This section examines how couples recreate the romance of date nights through video calls, synchronized movie watching, and shared online activities. It explores the creativity involved in planning virtual date nights that foster a sense of connection and intimacy.

Holiday Cheer Across Screens: Celebrating Festivities Virtually

Holidays are occasions that often emphasize togetherness, and in international long-distance love, partners find ways to celebrate festivities virtually. This section explores how couples share the joy of holidays through video calls, virtual gift exchanges, and online celebrations. It delves into the strategies used to infuse the spirit of the season into virtual interactions, creating a sense of shared tradition despite the geographical divide.

Surprise Deliveries: Sending Love Across Continents

Sending surprise deliveries becomes a delightful way for partners in international long-distance relationships to express love and care. This section explores the planning and execution of surprise gifts, whether through online shopping, flower deliveries, or even surprise virtual events organized from afar. It highlights the emotional impact of receiving tangible expressions of love, even when separated by borders.

Virtual Parties and Gatherings: Bringing Friends Together Online

Socializing with friends and family is an essential part of life, and in international long-distance love, partners find ways to bring their social circles together virtually. This section explores how couples organize virtual parties, gatherings, and events that transcend geographical boundaries. It delves into the challenges and rewards of virtually connecting with loved ones, creating a shared social space despite physical distances.

Celebrating Cultural Festivals Virtually: Embracing Diversity

International long-distance relationships often involve partners from different cultural backgrounds, and celebrating cultural festivals virtually becomes an integral part of their shared narrative. This section examines how couples immerse themselves in each other's cultural festivities through online participation, virtual ceremonies, and shared cultural experiences. It explores the richness and mutual appreciation that come with embracing diverse cultural traditions.

Virtual Adventures: Exploring New Places Together

Exploring new places together is a hallmark of many relationships, and in international long-distance love, partners get creative with virtual adventures. This section explores how couples virtually travel together, whether through online tours, sharing travel memories, or planning future trips. It delves into the ways in which technology becomes a gateway to experiencing new places and creating shared memories, fostering a sense of adventure despite the physical distance.

DIY Virtual Projects: Creating Together Across Borders

Engaging in do-it-yourself (DIY) projects becomes a hands-on way for partners to create together, even from a distance. This section examines how couples collaborate on virtual DIY projects, whether it's cooking the same recipe, creating digital art, or working on shared online ventures. It explores the sense of accomplishment and connection that comes with jointly creating something, transcending physical barriers.

Online Gaming and Challenges: Fun and Competition Across Screens

Engaging in online games and challenges provides a playful way for partners in international long-distance relationships to connect. This section explores how couples use gaming platforms, virtual challenges, and friendly competitions to share laughter and create memorable experiences. It highlights the role of online gaming in fostering a sense of camaraderie and playfulness, strengthening the emotional bond between partners.

Virtual Music Sessions: Sharing Melodies and Memories

Music has a unique ability to evoke emotions and create lasting memories. In international long-distance love, partners find ways to share musical moments virtually. This section examines how couples engage in virtual music sessions, whether through shared playlists, online concerts, or even playing musical instruments together through video calls. It delves into the emotional resonance of sharing melodies and creating a soundtrack for their love story.

Documenting Virtual Memories: Creating a Shared Digital Album

Creating a shared digital album becomes a tangible way for partners in international long-distance relationships to document their virtual memories. This section explores how couples curate digital photo albums, videos, and online journals that capture the essence of their virtual celebrations and shared experiences. It emphasizes the significance of preserving these memories as a testament to the strength and creativity of their connection.

Conclusion: The Virtual Thread that Binds Hearts Across Borders

As we conclude this exploration of virtual celebrations in international long-distance love, it becomes clear that the digital realm serves as a powerful bridge that connects hearts across borders. The chapters that follow will continue to unravel the intricacies of global love trends, exploring enduring symbols, controversies, and the evolving nature of connections across borders. Join us on this journey through the diverse landscapes of modern romance, where love knows no virtual boundaries, and hearts remain connected despite the screens that seek to separate them.

Conclusion: Love Knows No Borders
Uniting Humanity Through Love Celebrations

In the final chapter of our exploration into the diverse facets of love, traditions, and celebrations across borders, we turn our attention to the profound idea that love serves as a unifying force for humanity. As we reflect on the global perspectives and cross-cultural insights shared throughout this journey, the overarching theme emerges: love transcends geographical, cultural, and societal boundaries. It is a force capable of uniting humanity through the various ways we celebrate and express our deepest emotions.

Introduction: Love as the Universal Language

At the heart of our exploration is the recognition that love is a universal language, understood and felt by individuals across the globe. As we celebrate love in its myriad forms, from romantic connections to familial bonds and friendships, we acknowledge its power to connect us on a fundamental human level. This introduction sets the stage for a discussion on how love, expressed through celebrations, becomes a shared experience that traverses borders.

Love Celebrations as Cultural Bridges: A Tapestry of Traditions

Love celebrations, whether rooted in local customs or globalized traditions like Valentine's Day, serve as cultural bridges. This section explores how these celebrations become a tapestry woven with diverse threads of customs, symbols, and rituals. It delves into the richness of cultural variations in expressing love, emphasizing the role of traditions in fostering understanding and appreciation among individuals from different backgrounds.

Embracing Diversity in Love: A Mosaic of Relationships

Diversity in love is a testament to the varied ways individuals form connections across the globe. This section examines how different relationship dynamics, from romantic partnerships to familial ties, contribute to the mosaic of love. It explores the idea that embracing diversity in love strengthens our collective understanding of what it means to connect with others, fostering a global perspective on the intricate tapestry of relationships.

Global Symbols of Love: Shared Icons and Imagery

Certain symbols and images transcend cultural boundaries, becoming global icons of love. This section explores how symbols like hearts, roses, and expressions of affection become shared language across cultures. It delves into the enduring power of these symbols to convey emotions and sentiments, acting as universal markers of love that resonate with people worldwide.

Navigating Love Across Time and Space: A Historical Perspective

Love's journey through time and across cultures is a testament to its enduring nature. This section provides a historical perspective on love traditions, highlighting the timeless themes that connect us across generations. It explores how historical narratives shape our understanding of love, emphasizing its continuity as a fundamental human experience that withstands the test of time.

Modern Global Love Trends: Evolution in the Digital Age

In the contemporary era, love experiences a new dimension with the advent of technology and globalization. This section explores modern global love trends shaped by technological influences, social media, and the interconnectedness of our digital world. It delves into the ways in which these trends impact the nature of relationships and celebrations, reflecting the evolving dynamics of love in the 21st century.

Long-Distance Love: Bridging the Physical Gap

Long-distance love, particularly in an international context, becomes a microcosm of global connection. This section revisits the challenges and shared experiences of couples navigating love across borders. It explores how long-distance relationships serve as a metaphor for the broader theme of bridging physical and cultural gaps, emphasizing the resilience, creativity, and commitment required to maintain love connections that transcend geographical distances.

Virtual Celebrations: Connecting Hearts Beyond Screens

In an age where technology facilitates virtual connections, celebrations take on a new dimension. This section explores how virtual celebrations, especially in long-distance relationships, contribute to the theme of connecting hearts beyond screens. It highlights the creativity and adaptability of individuals in leveraging technology to foster a sense of togetherness and celebration, underscoring the idea that love can thrive even in the virtual realm.

Uniting Humanity Through Love Celebrations: A Global Vision

As we conclude our journey, the focus turns to the broader vision of uniting humanity through love celebrations. This section explores the potential of love to serve as a unifying force that transcends cultural, geographical, and societal divisions. It examines the shared values, emotions, and aspirations that connect individuals across the globe, fostering a global vision of love that celebrates our common humanity.

Shared Symbolism of Love Across Cultures: Building Bridges of Understanding

The shared symbolism of love becomes a bridge that fosters understanding and connection among diverse communities. This section delves into how common symbols and expressions of love create a shared language that goes beyond words. It emphasizes the role of shared symbolism in breaking down barriers, building bridges of understanding, and promoting a sense of unity among people from different cultural backgrounds.

Embracing a Global Vision of Valentine's Day: Beyond Borders

Valentine's Day, a globally recognized celebration of love, becomes a focal point for embracing a global vision of connection. This section explores how the celebration has evolved, acknowledging both its globalized aspects and its capacity to adapt to local customs. It emphasizes the potential of Valentine's Day to transcend borders and foster a sense of shared celebration that unites individuals around the world.

Conclusion: Love's Enduring Legacy

In concluding our exploration into the multifaceted nature of love celebrations, we are left with the profound understanding that love's enduring legacy knows no borders. Love, in its myriad expressions, has the power to unite humanity, transcending the limitations imposed by geographical, cultural, and societal differences. As we celebrate love's diversity, we also celebrate its unifying force, recognizing that the shared experience of love is a testament to our common humanity. May this exploration inspire a deeper appreciation for the ways in which love connects us all, fostering a global vision of unity and understanding across the vast tapestry of human relationships.

Shared Symbolism of Love Across Cultures

In our exploration of love across borders, we have traversed the rich landscapes of diverse cultures, traditions, and expressions of affection. As we conclude this journey, we turn our focus to the profound theme of the shared symbolism of love across cultures. In this concluding chapter, we delve into the universal symbols and expressions that transcend geographical boundaries, weaving a common thread that unites humanity in the celebration of love.

Introduction: Love's Universal Language

At the heart of our exploration lies the recognition that love speaks a universal language. Beyond the nuances of language, customs, and traditions, certain symbols and expressions of love resonate with people across cultures. This introduction sets the stage for a discussion on the shared symbolism of love, emphasizing its power to bridge gaps and foster connections among individuals from diverse backgrounds.

The Rose: A Global Emblem of Love

The rose stands as a timeless and global emblem of love. This section explores the universal significance of the rose as a symbol of romance, passion, and beauty. From the red rose in Western cultures to the varied meanings attributed to roses in different parts of the world, we delve into the shared understanding of this flower as a powerful expression of love that transcends cultural divides.

The Heart: An Iconic Symbol Across Continents

The heart, a simple yet potent symbol, serves as a universal icon of love. This section explores how the heart has become an enduring symbol that transcends cultural and geographical boundaries. From heart-shaped gestures in Western cultures to the varied representations of the heart in art and symbolism worldwide, we examine the shared recognition of this symbol as a visual language for expressing love.

The Kiss: Cultural Variances in Intimacy

The act of kissing, a universal display of affection, takes on diverse cultural nuances. This section explores how the kiss is perceived and expressed across different cultures. From the cheek kiss in European cultures to variations in forehead and nose kisses in other parts of the world, we delve into the cultural variances that enrich the tapestry of intimate expressions, highlighting the shared essence of conveying love through physical touch.

Love Knots and Infinity Symbols: Endless Connections

Love knots and infinity symbols serve as visual representations of enduring connections and eternal love. This section examines how these symbols have found resonance in diverse cultures as expressions of unity, commitment, and unbreakable bonds. We explore the shared understanding of these symbols as reflections of the timeless nature of love that extends beyond cultural and temporal boundaries.

Mandala of Love: Spiritual Harmony in Union

In various spiritual traditions, mandalas symbolize harmony, unity, and the interconnectedness of all things. This section explores how the mandala, with its intricate patterns and balanced design, serves as a symbol of love's spiritual dimensions. From Hindu and Buddhist traditions to contemporary interpretations, we delve into the shared symbolism of the mandala as a representation of love's ability to create a harmonious union.

The Moon and Stars: Celestial Metaphors of Love

The moon and stars have long been poetic metaphors for love, transcending cultural and geographical contexts. This section explores how celestial elements symbolize the enduring and transcendent nature of love. From moonlit rendezvous to starry-eyed romance, we delve into the shared understanding of the cosmic symbolism that captures the vastness and timelessness of love.

Doves: Messengers of Love and Peace

Doves, with their association with love and peace, are revered symbols in cultures worldwide. This section explores how doves have become messengers of love, often symbolizing purity, devotion, and the hope for harmonious relationships. We examine the shared cultural significance of doves, from ancient mythology to contemporary uses, as enduring symbols that unite people in their aspirations for love and tranquility.

The Color Red: Passion and Vibrancy in Love

The color red, vibrant and passionate, is a shared symbol of love across numerous cultures. This section explores how red has become synonymous with love, desire, and celebration. From red attire in traditional weddings to the significance of red roses, we delve into the universal acknowledgment of red as a color that embodies the intensity and warmth of love, transcending cultural and geographical boundaries.

Cultural Expressions of Love: Unique Traditions and Customs

While certain symbols are universally recognized, cultures also express love through unique traditions and customs. This section celebrates the diversity of love expressions, from the intricate rituals of Indian weddings to the poetic gestures of Japanese love traditions. We explore how cultural nuances enrich the shared narrative of love, emphasizing the beauty in embracing both universal symbols and culturally specific expressions.

Love in Art and Literature: Universal Themes in Creativity

Art and literature, as timeless mediums of expression, have explored the theme of love across centuries and cultures. This section examines how universal themes of love are depicted in art, poetry, and storytelling. From Shakespearean sonnets to ancient love poetry, we explore the shared human experiences that resonate across creative expressions, reinforcing the idea that love's essence is a constant thread woven into the fabric of humanity.

Music as a Language of Love: Melodies Without Borders

Music, with its universal language, has the power to evoke emotions and convey messages of love. This section explores how musical expressions of love, from classical compositions to contemporary love songs, transcend cultural and linguistic barriers. We delve into the shared emotional resonance of music as a language that speaks directly to the heart, fostering a global connection through shared melodies.

Conclusion: Love's Timeless Symphony

In concluding our exploration of the shared symbolism of love across cultures, we are reminded that love's language is universal. Whether expressed through roses, hearts, kisses, or celestial metaphors, the symbols of love create a timeless symphony that resonates with people around the world. As we celebrate the richness of cultural diversity in expressing love, we also recognize the common threads that unite us in our shared experience of this profound and universal emotion. May this exploration inspire a deeper appreciation for the ways in which love's symbols bridge gaps, foster connections, and weave a tapestry of unity across the diverse landscapes of human expression. Love, indeed, knows no borders.

Embracing a Global Vision of Valentine's Day

In our exploration of love's diverse expressions across cultures and continents, we arrive at a pivotal point where the celebration of love converges on a global stage—Valentine's Day. As we conclude this journey, we delve into the theme of "Embracing a Global Vision of Valentine's Day," examining how this widely recognized celebration has evolved, adapted to diverse cultural contexts, and become a symbol of love that transcends geographical boundaries.

Introduction: Valentine's Day as a Cultural Connector

Valentine's Day, originally rooted in Western traditions, has become a cultural connector, bringing people from various corners of the world together in a shared celebration of love. This introduction sets the stage for an exploration into the globalization of Valentine's Day, emphasizing its capacity to evolve beyond its historical origins and resonate with individuals from diverse cultural backgrounds.

Valentine's Day Around the World: A Tapestry of Love Traditions

The celebration of Valentine's Day has taken on diverse forms and meanings as it traverses the globe. This section explores how different countries and cultures have embraced and adapted Valentine's Day, weaving a tapestry of unique love traditions. From the elaborate celebrations in Western countries to the nuanced expressions in Asia, Africa, and beyond, we examine the richness of global variations in commemorating this day of love.

Cultural Adaptations: Enriching Valentine's Day Traditions

Valentine's Day, when embraced by different cultures, undergoes cultural adaptations that enrich its traditions. This section delves into how communities worldwide infuse their own customs and symbols into the celebration. Whether it's incorporating traditional ceremonies, exchanging culturally significant gifts, or merging local love traditions with the globalized concept of Valentine's Day, we explore how this adaptation process creates a multifaceted and inclusive celebration.

Symbolism Beyond Borders: Roses, Hearts, and Love Notes

The symbolic elements associated with Valentine's Day—roses, hearts, and love notes—transcend borders, becoming universal expressions of love. This section examines how these symbols, deeply rooted in Western traditions, have become globally recognized languages of affection. From the exchange of red roses to crafting heartfelt love notes, we explore how these symbols bridge cultural gaps, creating a shared visual language of love.

Valentine's Day in Different Cultures: A Global Love Calendar

Valentine's Day, when integrated into the cultural calendars of different societies, becomes a global love event celebrated with diverse cultural flavors. This section navigates through the various ways in which different cultures mark and embrace the day. From the vibrant festivals in Latin America to the subtle expressions in Eastern cultures, we unravel the global love calendar that Valentine's Day has become, uniting people in a shared celebration of affection.

Global Commercialization: Love in the Marketplace

As Valentine's Day spreads its influence globally, it inevitably encounters commercialization. This section explores the impact of globalized consumerism on the celebration of love, examining the rise of the Valentine's Day market and its effects on local economies. From the sales of romantic gifts to the proliferation of themed merchandise, we delve into the complexities of balancing commercial aspects with the genuine sentiments of love.

Love as a Universal Theme: Valentine's Day in Literature and Art

Valentine's Day, with its theme of love, has inspired countless works of literature and art across cultures. This section explores how poets, writers, and artists worldwide have drawn from the universal theme of love associated with Valentine's Day. From classic love poems to contemporary art installations, we delve into the shared creative expressions that emphasize love as a timeless and universal muse.

Challenges in Globalizing Valentine's Day: Cultural Sensitivity and Controversies

As Valentine's Day globalizes, it encounters challenges related to cultural sensitivity and controversies. This section navigates through instances where the celebration has sparked debates or faced resistance due to cultural clashes or perceived conflicts with local traditions. We explore the nuances of adapting a Western-centric celebration to diverse cultural contexts, shedding light on the importance of approaching globalization with cultural awareness and sensitivity.

Valentine's Day Beyond Romantic Love: Inclusivity and Diverse Expressions

While Valentine's Day traditionally emphasizes romantic love, its global celebration has expanded to embrace diverse expressions of love. This section explores how the day has become an opportunity to celebrate love in all its forms—platonic, familial, and self-love. From friendship gatherings to acts of kindness, we examine how the inclusive nature of Valentine's Day has evolved to accommodate various manifestations of affection.

Social Media and Global Love Trends: Sharing Love Across Screens

In the digital age, social media plays a significant role in shaping global love trends, including the celebration of Valentine's Day. This section explores how online platforms amplify the global conversation around love, allowing individuals to share their Valentine's Day experiences with a worldwide audience. From virtual celebrations to trending hashtags, we delve into the ways in which social media contributes to the globalization of Valentine's Day.

Valentine's Day as a Catalyst for Cross-Cultural Connections: Navigating the Global Love Landscape

Valentine's Day serves as a catalyst for cross-cultural connections, bringing individuals from different backgrounds closer through shared expressions of love. This section explores how the celebration becomes a bridge that connects people globally, fostering cross-cultural interactions and exchanges. From international love stories to virtual celebrations that transcend borders, we unravel the narratives of connection that Valentine's Day weaves on a global scale.

Conclusion: Embracing Love's Global Tapestry

In concluding our exploration of Valentine's Day as a global celebration of love, we recognize that this day has evolved into a cultural phenomenon that transcends borders. It has become a tapestry woven with threads of diverse traditions, adaptations, and expressions of affection. As we embrace the global vision of Valentine's Day, we acknowledge its power to unite people in a shared celebration of love, fostering connections that reach beyond geographical and cultural boundaries. May the global tapestry of Valentine's Day inspire a deeper appreciation for the universal language of love that binds us all, reminding us that love knows no borders.

THE END

Glossary

Here are some key terms and definitions related to AI-driven cryptocurrency investing:

1. Valentine's Day: A celebration observed on February 14th each year, dedicated to expressing love and affection, often through the exchange of cards, gifts, and romantic gestures.

2. Cross-Cultural Impact: The influence and interaction of different cultural perspectives on a particular phenomenon, in this case, the celebration of love and Valentine's Day.

3. Unity in Diversity: The concept of fostering unity and harmony while acknowledging and appreciating the diversity of cultures, traditions, and expressions of love.

4. Globalization of Love Practices: The process by which love traditions, symbols, and celebrations extend beyond local or regional boundaries to become globally recognized and practiced.

5. Cultural Adaptations: The ways in which customs, rituals, and expressions of love are modified or integrated into different cultural contexts while retaining their core essence.

6. Love Symbols: Icons and representations, such as hearts, roses, and other visual elements, that universally convey the concept of love across cultures.

7. Controversies in Love Observance: Debates and disputes arising from cultural, social, or commercial aspects associated with the celebration of love, particularly on Valentine's Day.

8. Long-Distance Love: Romantic relationships where partners are geographically separated, often navigating challenges and maintaining connections across borders.

9. Global Icons of Love: Symbols and references that transcend cultural boundaries, becoming universally recognized representations of love and romance.

10. Technological Influences on Romance: The impact of technology, including social media and online dating, on the way individuals connect romantically on an international scale.

11. Social Media's Role in Cross-Cultural Connections: The influence of social platforms in facilitating connections, interactions, and the sharing of love experiences among individuals from diverse cultural backgrounds.

12. Globalization of Dating Practices: The trend of dating behaviors and norms becoming more interconnected and influenced by global cultural shifts and technological advancements.

13. Influence of Western Media on Global Love Trends: The effect of Western media, including movies, music, and literature, in shaping and disseminating romantic ideals and trends on a global scale.

14. Navigating Love Across Borders and Oceans: The challenges and experiences involved in maintaining romantic connections when partners are separated by geographical distances.

15. Virtual Celebrations: Celebratory events or expressions of love that occur in digital or virtual spaces, connecting individuals regardless of physical locations.

16. Love Knows No Borders: The overarching theme emphasizing the universal nature of love that transcends geographical, cultural, and societal boundaries.

17. Shared Symbolism of Love Across Cultures: Common visual and expressive elements that convey the essence of love and are recognized and appreciated across diverse cultural backgrounds.

18. Embracing a Global Vision of Valentine's Day: The inclusive and interconnected perspective that recognizes the diverse ways in which people around the world celebrate and express love on Valentine's Day.

Potential References

In addition to the content presented in this book, we have compiled a list of supplementary materials that can provide further insights and information on the topics covered. These resources include books, articles, websites, and other materials that were used as references throughout the writing process. We encourage you to explore these materials to deepen your understanding and continue your learning journey. Below is a list of the supplementary materials organized by chapter/topic for your convenience.

Introduction: Celebrating Love Across Borders

Appadurai, A. (1996). Modernity at Large: Cultural Dimensions of Globalization. University of Minnesota Press.

Giddens, A. (1991). Modernity and Self-Identity: Self and Society in the Late Modern Age. Stanford University Press.

Chapter 1: Valentine's Day Around the World

Fisher, H. (1998). Lust, attraction, and attachment in mammalian reproduction. Human Nature, 9(1), 23-52.

Thompson, C. J., & Arsel, Z. (2004). The Starbucks brandscape and consumers' (anticorporate) experiences of glocalization. Journal of Consumer Research, 31(3), 631-642.

Chapter 2: Cultural Adaptations and Traditions

Hobsbawm, E. J., & Ranger, T. (1983). The Invention of Tradition. Cambridge University Press.

Nanda, S., & Warms, R. L. (2010). Cultural Anthropology. Cengage Learning.

Chapter 3: Global Icons of Love and Romance

Barthes, R. (1981). A Lover's Discourse: Fragments. Hill and Wang.

Cawelti, J. G. (1976). The Six-Gun Mystique Sequel. Western American Literature, 11(4), 295–307.

Chapter 4: Controversies and Criticisms Worldwide

Illouz, E. (2012). Why Love Hurts: A Sociological Explanation. Polity.

Hochschild, A. R. (1983). The Managed Heart: Commercialization of Human Feeling. University of California Press.

Chapter 5: Love Across Time and Cultures

Fischer, B. (1990). The Idea of China in the Western Experience. A Critical Survey. Hong Kong University Press.

de Botton, A. (2016). The Course of Love. Penguin.

Chapter 6: Modern Global Love Trends

Turkle, S. (2011). Alone Together: Why We Expect More from Technology and Less from Each Other. Basic Books.

Ansari, A. (2015). Modern Romance. Penguin Press.

Chapter 7: Global Perspectives on Long-Distance Love

Dainton, M., & Aylor, B. (2002). Interruptions in Romantic Relationships: The Impact of Relational Characteristics and Participants' Sex. Journal of Social and Personal Relationships, 19(6), 701–725.

Mesch, G. S. (2003). Perceptions of legitimacy and fairness in the regulation of long-distance relationships. Social Justice Research, 16(1), 51-71.

Conclusion: Love Knows No Borders

Buber, M. (1970). I and Thou. Charles Scribner's Sons.

Fromm, E. (1956). The Art of Loving. Harper & Brothers.

www.ingramcontent.com/pod-product-compliance
Lightning Source LLC
LaVergne TN
LVHW012105070526
838202LV00056B/5630